UNDERSTANDING PHILOSOPHY

Books by James K. Feibleman

DEATH OF THE GOD IN MEXICO
CHRISTIANITY, COMMUNISM AND THE IDEAL SOCIETY
IN PRAISE OF COMEDY
POSITIVE DEMOCRACY
THE MARGITIST
INTRODUCTION TO PEIRCE'S PHILOSOPHY
JOURNEY TO THE COASTAL MARSH
THE REVIVAL OF REALISM
THE THEORY OF HUMAN CULTURE
THE LONG HABIT
AESTHETICS
TREMBLING PRAIRIE
THE DARK BIFOCALS
ONTOLOGY
THE INSTITUTIONS OF SOCIETY
INSIDE THE GREAT MIRROR
THE PIOUS SCIENTIST
RELIGIOUS PLATONISM
BIOSOCIAL FACTORS IN MENTAL ILLNESS
FOUNDATIONS OF EMPIRICISM
MANKIND BEHAVING
THE TWO-STORY WORLD
GREAT APRIL
MORAL STRATEGY
THE REACH OF POLITICS
THE WAY OF A MAN
THE QUIET REBELLION
SCIENTIFIC METHOD

Co-Author of

SCIENCE AND THE SPIRIT OF MAN
THE UNLIMITED COMMUNITY
WHAT SCIENCE REALLY MEANS

UNDERSTANDING PHILOSOPHY
A Popular History of Ideas

JAMES K. FEIBLEMAN

HORIZON PRESS  New York

For Ira and Bop Freeman

Preface

Over the years people have often asked me, "What is philosophy? Can you recommend a simple account that I could understand without special training? I know nothing at all about philosophy but I often feel that there must be something in it for me."

This book was written for them.

New Orleans
April 1973

Contents

10   *Contents*

Chapter I

The Uses of Philosophy

Philosophy is a difficult subject that uses ordinary words in queer ways and has no practical application whatsoever.

That at any rate is what most people suppose today. And they do so because they forget that philosophy is a technical field. People who would not try to understand physics or mathematics because of the special signs and symbols employed are misled into thinking that philosophy is readily understandable because the words are recognizable. In this sense philosophy has been misleading. For it makes up its technical vocabulary by the extraordinary ways in which it uses ordinary words.

It requires some trouble to understand philosophy, but it is worth the trouble simply because philosophy is one of the most useful enterprises ever undertaken by man. It won't build bridges but it will organize new information. As everyone knows, in our lifetime there have been tremendous advances in human knowledge. The radio, television, the airplane, psychoanalysis, the new "wonder" drugs and other biochemical marvels, the new physics and technology, including relativity physics and quantum mechanics, are just a few. Along with the new knowledge have come new challenges, such as the challenge of international trade (the European Common Market) and international Communism.

These new developments have brought new problems with them, some trivial, some grave. But most of all they have presented the average citizen with a spectacle of the greatest confusion. All lines run away from the center and there seems to be no common ground. No one stops to think that it is the business of philosophy to bring clarity and consistency into all this confusion and to give the individual somewhere to stand while all the various new theoretical and practical advances swirl around him.

The uses of philosophy are both individual and social. Let us begin with the individual uses.

The first of these is the satisfaction of simple curiosity. Man shares with the lower animals a great desire to know about things. The same urge that impels a monkey to examine a stick by turning it over motivates a man to satisfy his inquiry, but in the case of man the urge is much more extensive. Man's curiosity is extended backward and forward in time and throughout space; it includes the relations between things as well as the things themselves. It is bounded only by the limitations of the individual.

From infancy to maturity man goes through two well-recognized stages: innocence and innocence lost. It is no news to anyone that children begin life in a state of innocence, but most people forget that a child's is not an empty innocence, but an innocence full of curiosity.

I was seven years old when I saw a man die. I was playing in the front yard one summer morning watching a man on a ladder paint the side of the house across the street. All of a sudden he fell to the ground and lay there very still. His family rushed out and stood around weeping and wailing.

Since it was very strange and considerably frightening, I turned back into my house and hunted for my mother.

"I have just seen a man die," I announced.

"I know," she said. "I was hoping you would not know about that until later."

"Will that happen to me?"

She smiled. "Not for a very, very long time."

"Will that happen to me?" I repeated.

"Not until you have grown up and become a man and lived your life and grown very old, and then perhaps you won't mind so much."

"But it will happen to me?"

"Yes."

"Well, then," I said, "I don't think I want to go on at all. I would rather go back to where I started."

A quizzical smile came over her face. "I'm afraid that's rather impossible."

She sent me out to play again. But I went downstairs and tried to understand my predicament. I felt I was in an awful fix and I didn't understand how it had happened.

There is nothing stronger than the curiosity of children. They are eager to learn about everything, and they routinely ask the embarrassingly fundamental questions that adults are never able to answer: What is God like, how big is space, what is time? If philosophy has any native home, it is in the questions of children. Their state of innocence is not after all so innocent. They know what questions to ask.

But we don't know what to answer. Yet we answer just the same, giving definite answers to fundamentally unanswerable questions. Our children may not be content with the stock replies formulated by dead authorities, drawn from religion, philosophy, and politics by teachers and parents generally, but they know that they must accept them, and so with a shrug they go off to think about something else.

And the rest of their adult lives are spent in the small business of everyday: running for buses, shaving and bathing, paying taxes, making a living, getting along with family, friends, and associates. It all takes up most of the available time. At night they are too tired to think and only want to be amused because amusement is restful. And so the childish philosophical questions are never raised again. Anyhow, there would be no point, since now they have found out exactly what has to be done to get along. This is innocence lost.

A few, a very few, however, take a third step, to innocence regained. They are more sensitive than the rest, or more stubborn, I do not know which. They reject the answers that were made to their childish questions, but they keep the questions. From this tiny group come all the productive and original people among us, the artists and philosophers who through their efforts make up the social world in which we live.

Thanks to them, human progress does not consist in finding the answers and so ending the search, but in adjustment to the search itself. At its highest, life is a perpetual inquiry. We live by the results but we are never satisfied with them, and so while we accept them in order to exist, at the same time we endeavor to continue the inquiry. All men are by nature inquisitive, but some make a profession of inquiry. A philosophy is the working tool of inquisitive men. "I would," said Democritus, "rather discover one cause than gain the kingdom of Persia." The vast discoveries connected with the atom in recent physics no doubt owe their origin to the early Greek philosophers who were the first to think about the possibilities of such discoveries.

In addition to wanting to know, the individual has things he wants to do, goals he would like to reach. But unless some consistent plan is followed, he may defeat himself. He may be undoing with his left hand what he is endeavoring to do with his right, without ever understanding that this is the case. He may, for instance, want the high regard of his fellows but cheat them in order to gain it, and they in their turn may be so confused about values as to admire the success he has made in this way. Philosophy can facilitate a forward progress in achievement through action by formulating a life pattern in which the individual can measure his progress and correct his direction. By using his philosophical compass he can keep from going off course.

Human beings can conduct their lives only in terms of some kind of framework. They are incapable of merely existing in a helter-skelter world. The framework is usually presented to them by a currently fashionable and dominant institution—a church or a state. But what is presented in this way is nothing more or less than philosophy. At some point it was the work of philosophers attempting to solve some of the recurrent problems of philosophy. The framework may be a myth, which is after all only a story told in symbols evoking emotions and regarded as true, as with a religion. Or the framework may be a kind of economic law, in which case it presents itself as the inevitable consequences of some basic facts, Marxism for instance. But in any case it is a framework, a philosophy imbedded in the nature of things and indispensable to people.

One of the most important branches of philosophy is ethics, the theory of the good. Morality consists in socially adopted ethics. Men tend to think of morality as a curbing of the sexual impulse. But this is a negative side. There is a positive side which is more important and all-embracing: how one wishes to conduct oneself toward oneself as well as toward one's fellows. What ought one to do, what should one seek? These are typical moral questions. The composition of a life-plan is moral, and the following of it is, too.

Morality tends to lend depth to practice, to make of the activities of existence a wholly concrete affair having definite dimensions. The life of a man is fuller if he knows what life is. This is not to say, of course, that life should be rigid. Any comprehensive plan must have some elasticity, some allowance for change. But to know in general where one wants to go—there is nothing confining about that. Morality is a set of laws that one sets up for oneself. Some laws are constrictive, but others add new freedom, and it is the latter kind that we are talking about. Prohibition was restrictive; it forbade everyone to drink alcohol, even the majority who knew how to control their amount. But traffic lights make it possible to cross an intersection faster.

The chief business of philosophy so far as the individual is concerned is to intensify life. And what it can do for the individual generally it can do for him in connection with any of his enterprises. This need not be understood in any high and mighty sense. Philosophy is useful in backing up the activities of each day. Jurisprudence—the philosophy of law—is capable of intensifying the meaning of law for the ordinary citizen as well as for the practicing lawyer or judge. The philosophy of science lends depth to the experience of the research scientist, and it seems as though all of the great scientists have had an intense interest in this direction. Einstein, for instance, physicist though he was, had studied philosophy and been influenced by it. Behind every great physicist there has stood the philosophy he acquired in his early training.

If it is the business of philosophy to intensify life, there is no place in which it does so as directly as in the appreciation of art. Art is in a way everybody's profession. To see the world as an artist does means only to see it personally. The philosophy of art is called esthetics. It takes some knowledge of esthetics to appreciate the grandeur and depth in great works of art. But esthetics has another and more personal contribution to make for the individual. A study of the philosophy of art leads to an intensification of the senses. Those who have learned something of the theory of art can feel more deeply than others; they have found out how to probe the complexities of their experience, and as a consequence they lead a richer life.

But the use of philosophy by the individual is very far from the whole of philosophy's practical program. There are the social uses to be considered as well.

One great use of philosophy is to establish social organizations on some kind of permanent basis. The amount of philosophy involved depends partly on the size of the social organization.

For an institution, a charter is required in order to secure stability. In a charter the philosophy may be implicit or explicit

—implicit as in the articles of incorporation of an industrial company with the common law philosophy, or explicit as in the Roman Catholic Church with the philosophy of Thomas Aquinas.

A social philosophy consists in a set of principles or laws which demand adherence to the belief in their truth. By this method they offer a stable basis which can keep the individual members together and so preserve the society. Men who hold a set of beliefs in common will endeavor to work together better than they would without it, and the more fundamental the beliefs the better the work.

In the last world war when France was defeated and occupied by the Germans, there existed a strong underground movement of men working for the liberation of their country from its oppressors. To make secure such a difficult effort, a philosophy was needed—not just any system of ideas but one that fitted the peculiar situation. Fortunately, such a philosophy existed. In Jean-Paul Sartre's version of existentialism reality was wholly individual and hung on the feeling of nausea which told the individual that he was an individual, and on the moment of decision which told him that the ultimate responsibility for himself was his own. Now the members of the underground could not of course find many opportunities to congregate. They had lost their social self-respect through the defeat of their country in war, and each had to maintain it for himself. Existentialism was perfectly suited to the situation.

For a society something more is required, for the social organization is larger and a great many more people are involved. One thinks immediately of the American society, and of the philosophy which helped to establish it formally, a philosophy contained in the American Declaration of Independence and the Constitution of the United States. This is easily identified as derived from the philosophy of John Locke and Montesquieu. The philosophy of the Soviet Union, as everyone knows, was chosen deliberately and adopted formally.

For man's largest organization, a culture or civilization, the philosophy is so pervasive that it is difficult to define in any particular case. But certainly in Western civilization, the institutions which it contains have so much in common that it is easy to suppose that they have underlying assumptions. The dynamism of Western civilization is well known and so is the belief in the method of science. The perfectability of this world relies upon both and contains its own system of ideas.

In the struggle between societies for survival or supremacy, philosophy, then, can be a weapon. We are engaged in an immense struggle with the forces of Communism in Soviet Russia and Communist China. They use philosophy as an instrument of propaganda. We use aid in various forms to undeveloped countries. We send them industrial products and farm products. Why don't we send them the philosophy of democracy as well? Not just the forms but the substance. It is not reasonable to expect other people to follow our democratic procedures without telling them why such procedures should be followed. Many countries have tried to copy the democracy which has worked so well in England, France, and the United States, but they failed because they adopted the practices without absorbing the philosophy. They *follow* democracy but they make no attempt to *understand* it. To practice democracy successfully it is necessary to comprehend the democratic philosophy.

In addition to the philosophical imports of American democracy, there are of course peculiarly American developments, such as the multiple-party system. Why does it work so well, why is it flexible yet steady, providing for changes within a system which does not itself materially change?

The philosophers who occupy themselves with politics could help here. They are needed to provide an understanding accompanying the changes in policy and principle which are bound to occur in any dynamic society. Even more, they are needed to argue in defense of the system against those who suppose it to be wrong. We are quickly learning that the mild little fellow, the academician who teaches, thinks, experiments, or writes the pure theory of his field, may pack a punch when his theories come to be applied. We have learned this about the physicist, the chemist, even the biologist. But we have not learned it yet about the philosopher. In the struggle with international Communism, the philosophers of democracy could be potent weapons. Why don't we use them more?

Perhaps it will be easier to explain how to use philosophy if for a start we go back to its beginnings in ancient Greece and then follow its adventures through the history of Europe until we come up to its position in the world today. This will help us to understand just what philosophy is by watching its development as it struggled to become what it is, and as it influenced, and was influenced by, the course of history.

Chapter II

Before the Coming
of the Greeks

Philosophy as a separate topic began with the Greeks. But the interest itself, the random thoughts in the field that the Greeks later gave a name to, had a much earlier history. How early we do not know.

Certainly the first animals that could be called men must have paused briefly after they had eaten enough for the day to wonder about the nature of things. They did not have much time for that kind of question, however, because they did not know how to store food for future needs and so had to forage or hunt continually. They could gather edible seeds and wild grasses but there were also enemies to be dealt with, both animal and human. The animals were much bigger then, the mammoth, the woolly rhinoceros and other hardy beasts found grazing along the margins of the European ice-sheet, and the defenses against them were much weaker. Yet the sense of wonder persisted and would not be downed. It was probably nourished by perilous events, such as thunder storms, and the omnipresence of death.

The records of these events, if ever there were any, are lost.

If early man was able to take any time away from his struggle for existence and survival in order to consider his predicament, as he most probably did, we have found no account of it. What we have found are hunting tools; they are very primitive—chopper-tools, and hand-axes, and much later, spearheads. Inscriptions on bone and ivory and drawings on cave walls are very much later indeed. Still, they are all that we have. What they show chiefly is men hunting.

They bred no animals, grew no plants, and had to be continually on the move to catch or collect enough food for their support, and this took them in small groups over a wide area. There was little chance to accumulate possessions and little time to devote to anything that did not contribute to their immediate survival.

It is toward the end rather than near the beginning of man's forty thousand years in his present state that we find the first signs of his curiosity about the meaning of the human condition.

It is possible from cave art to discover some of his earliest beliefs. The drawings on cave walls were designed primarily as aids in hunting, to point the directions in which game could be found or to insure the success of the hunt by imitative magic. In this way he was able to see himself and his animals in a single environment in which each played an essential part. The beginnings of an intensive self-awareness are certainly already present, marked by articles of personal adornment if by nothing else.

There is some evidence of religious practices in the remains of burials. Graves have been found cut into rock floors, and bodies that were buried ringed with stones or with pairs of antlers of the mountain goat. That there was any formality at all would indicate the presence of some sort of religious belief concerning the possibility of a life after death.

I have often talked about what I call the four grand routes of inquiry the way in which men have expressed their wonder about the nature of things. They are: art, religion, philosophy and science. Works of art and religious customs date back so early that we do not know which came first, but we do know that they had practical purposes. Prayers for rain, dances for the fertility of crops and women, invocations for success in hunting, called on both imitative art and religious magic. It took many thousands of years before these developed into the fine arts—art for the sake of art—and the organized religions, including worship without a personal motive. In these last instances there are elements of curiosity, attempts to discover through activities and emotions what life is all about.

The first two grand routes of inquiry, art and religion, could be as much as forty thousand years old, as old as man in his present stage, that is. Then suddenly, between three thousand and twenty-five hundred years ago, the Greek people discovered a new form of inquiry into the nature of things, a form which could operate by means of human reasoning. This they called philosophy, and it was an offshoot of religion. In the seventeenth century of our era a fourth form appeared, one that undertook to unite all three of the human faculties in the name of experimental science, this time an offshoot of philosophy.

We have had all four grand routes of inquiry with us since science joined the others only a few hundred years ago. It has had so many dazzling successes that it has tended to obscure everything else. But art, religion and philosophy are still with us and are likely to be for some time. What we often forget is that we need new varieties of religion. New varieties of art continue to be discovered, and—as I hope to show in this book—new varieties of philosophy as well.

Most of the advances in civilization have been toward the intensification of efforts stemming from conflicting motives. Primitive man's power for good and bad was strictly limited. Ours is much more effective. But it lies in many of the same directions. Primitive man wanted to help and hurt his fellows, he wanted to help the members of his own group and hurt the others. We have not changed that much even today. It has happened that the groups on both sides have grown much larger, and our inventions are all in the direction of complexity. On the good side, instead of medicine men—*shamans*, they were called

—we have hospitals and doctors; on the other side, instead of warriors with spears we have bombers with an atomic arsenal; but the division is still the same.

Only two enterprises have not advanced in the same way, and by their very nature they cannot and perhaps even should not. Both art and philosophy remain their early selves. It is the nature of both to make every effort to get back to the simplest beginnings. The less taken for granted the better. Let us consider them separately for the moment.

Artists have seen and said this from their own point of view. In recent times, for instance, the great French painter Cézanne said that he was trying to describe on his canvases his own sensations in the presence of nature. Similarly, the Swiss painter Klee said that he wanted to begin with a tiny formal motif, the smallest possible.

The philosophers have much the same ambition. They do not want to have to move loaded down with all the inherited baggage of their predecessors but to make a fresh start each time, taking nothing at all for granted but what the world forces upon their naive perceptions and thoughts. That is why, although they cover eventually much the same ground, they start from places widely removed from each other and so they tend to organize things quite differently.

No development ever comes entirely from nothing. Probably the suggestions which led eventually to philosophy came from the earliest organized religious beliefs. Around the world religious speculation centered on different aspects of human interest. In Palestine it concerned itself with God; in India it concerned itself with the innermost self; in China it concerned itself with social life and the human community; in Greece it concerned itself with the nature of the physical world. How the self and the community developed can be learned by a study of Indian and Chinese philosophies. It will be seen that they followed the respective dominant religions closely. Not so with the Greeks.

We shall examine in this book only the last of the four—Greek thought as it influenced western civilization in Europe and the Americas. And we shall find that, unlike the thought of India and China, it went its own way, apart from religion.

Probably ancient Egypt furnished it with the earliest clues. The animal gods which had dominated Egyptian religious thought were finally replaced by the sun-god, Rē. The strongest hint of things to come in the way of thought was indicated by the symbolic representation of the gods, and of these the sun-god, Rē, was the most significant, since a single god meant an ultimate deity. When in 1375 B.C. Amenhotep IV (or Ikhnaton) proclaimed that henceforth not Amon-Rē but Aton was to be worshipped as a monotheistic deity represented by the solar disk, he set the forces at work which were to move in the direction of further abstraction.

It was a short distance in human thought from the sun to "light," as represented by one aspect of existence, and on to a final and absolute being which is the source of everything; big steps but more easily taken because of the big first step. Jewish belief in a single god who was responsible for the creation of the world was certainly much older, but the Greek historian Herodotus was familiar only with the Egyptian, and in fact he traced the influence of the earlier Egyptian gods on the catalogue of Greek gods. The thought that the idea of unity could be found in anything other than a god was left to the early Greeks to discover.

The Egyptians had the idea of a divine order into which all created things were fitted as soon as they had come into existence. This could be done because all things are made of one substance and so substitutions were easy to accomplish. All of this could be represented in symbols. A man's place in society continued after his death, and, if the dead wanted his daily bread as he had had it when living, it could be a wooden representation of a loaf which was left at his tomb. It was not the person who was important, anyhow, but his spirit, which was detachable from him and which acted for him.

In all of these efforts we can detect the tremendous efforts the

Egyptians made to reach a kind of knowledge which was not applicable to them only but was universal. There was in Egyptian history more than the traces of a hard materialism which sought an explanation of natural forces—and human forces, too —apart from religious influences. The ideas of natural justice and morality had existed for some time. In the Old Kingdom for instance the emphasis had been on the good life in this world, and it was in a later period that great importance was attached to life after death, which is of course the Egypt we know best. Egyptian thought left no permanent landmarks in philosophy but it may have been these elements in Egyptian culture which suggested philosophy to the Greeks.

Chapter III

The Earliest
Greek Philosophers

Philosophy as we know it was first thought of in ancient Greece. The land we call Greece, the country which you will find pointing down into the Mediterranean between Italy to the west and Turkey to the east, has been there for a long time, inhabited by more or less the same people. Where the Greeks came from no one knows. There is a theory that the white race moved down through the Caucasus, between the Caspian and the Black seas, into what is now Turkey, and from there turned west into southern Europe, but nobody is certain. They overcame a small native population living in Greece already, and imposed their own language.

The Greeks did not call themselves "Greek," by the way, but "Hellenes," because they considered themselves descendants of Helen of Troy, the subject of so much fighting in Homer's *Iliad*, in which there is also an account of many Greek religious beliefs. We say "Greek," but we often use the term "Hellenic" to refer to the civilization. If we know nothing else about the early Greeks, we know at least that they had the most burning curiosity of any people anywhere ever. They wanted to know not just how things were then but how they are always. They had a name for their kind of curiosity, they called it "philosophy," which means "love of wisdom," and they meant by it the search for general knowledge. They wanted to know, for instance, whether all men are mortal, not merely whether a man named Socrates was mortal. And they saw that if you knew the first, you could find the second from it.

They were not reasonable in everything, however. The Greek city-states invariably fought with one another. The year after Solon, the Greek law-giver, was responsible for a sacred war to protect the shrine of Apollo at Delphi (595 B.C.) he was elected to high office at Athens. In 445 the two principal city-states, Athens and Sparta, agreed to a thirty years' peace, Athens recognizing the hegemony of Sparta in the Peleponnesus, Sparta recognizing the maritime confederacy of Delos, but a mere fourteen years later war broke out again between them.

Once upon a time, the Greeks had one of the greatest civilizations ever heard of, perhaps the greatest that was ever developed by a small population. By the fifth century B.C. Greece was a collection of independent city-states, small cities by present estimates. The most important of them was Athens, a city of only some 250,000 free people, but with a considerable number of slaves. There were other cities of comparable size, such as Sparta and Corinth, but Athens was the home of the greatest number of geniuses.

It is amazing to consider what we owe to those Athenians. Remember of course that most of them were businessmen, chiefly manufacturers and traders. The others, though few in number, invented the theatre, democracy, history, the sciences, and made great contributions to the arts, especially to painting, sculpture and music. Most of the paintings have been lost, but we still have some of the sculpture. Their architecture was so good that it has been imitated ever since. Some of their buildings and temples still stand. Above all, perhaps, they invented philosophy, a way of thinking that has the greatest usefulness.

They were responsible for so much of civilization that it is perhaps easier to make a list of what we have that we do *not* owe to them. Experimental science was Greek but it was several thousands of years later before Europeans found out that the discoveries of science could be accumulated, so that every new scientist builds on the work of his predecessors. The Greeks had music but the Europeans were to add polyphonic music, compositions in which a number of melodies are played at the same time. The Greeks had *direct* democracy, with every citizen voting on every important issue, but this would be possible only in a very small country. In one containing millions of citizens everyone would not vote on everything and have the time to do anything else. So the Europeans worked out what we now call *representative* democracy, in which we vote for the men who do our voting for us.

What the Greeks seemed to have in abundance was curiosity. They inquired into all things, and not always just for practical purposes, either. For they seem to have learned two important tricks. One is that inquiry can be formalized and in that way be more effective. The other is that explanations which consist in pure theories without any practical motive can in their turn prove to be of the utmost practicality. Thus you might say that they discovered both pure theories and their practical importance.

We know very little about the earliest philosophers, who were among the earliest Greeks, but the little we do know is very exciting. They wrote a lot but only a few fragments of their work remain. From those fragments, however, we are able to reconstruct something of their interests and ideas.

The earliest philosophers wanted to understand themselves and the world in which they lived. Now, to try to understand *everything* is to practice philosophy. Still they were not idle dreamers. Many of them were successful businessmen who had made fortunes, while others had wide political influence.

From this distance we can see what they were working on better than they could, for they were too close. Many of them were trying to find the simplest materials of which the world is made, because to them the simplest materials were also the simplest things. Perhaps also, they thought, the simplest materials might be the causes of the more complex. And so their earliest investigations were of the physical world.

The simplest materials at that time and for many centuries later were thought to be four in number: earth, air, fire and water, familiar things found everywhere. Particular men selected particular ones of these: Xenophanes chose earth, Anaximenes preferred air, Thales selected water, and Heraclitus fire. In choosing one material and setting it above the others, each was sure he had found what is essential.

If you want to try for a new explanation of the world you have to reject the ones you find already established in your society. The best place to look for a philosophy which everyone accepts and nobody questions is in a church.

Xenophanes was the first man we know to have the courage to attack the ideas imbedded in the popular religion of his day. He did so for the reason that such attacks are always made: because religious ideas are usually the result of accepting unproved statements and embracing beliefs founded only on their emotional appeal. Such an attack is upsetting and most believers resent it. For even though religions conflict in a way which means not all of them can be right, very few believers take the trouble to make this discovery. Then, too, faith is comforting and doubt disturbing; all faiths, for that matter, are equally comforting, and that is what makes philosophers so suspicious of the ultimate truth of any one faith.

We have no record of how Xenophanes' views were received by the people among whom he lived. Perhaps they had already lost their beliefs and were ready for a change; perhaps not. We just do not know. Suffice to say that his opinions have a very modern ring. He remarked once that if horses could paint they would draw gods like horses, and he pointed out how shameful was the behavior of the gods as reported by Homer's epic poems. If there is a god, Xenophanes concluded, he is probably not like men in any respect.

Anaximenes explained everything in terms of the density of air, and he regarded the world as perishable. If there was always a world it was not necessarily always the same one. He knew enough to understand that the stars move round the earth, but he did not think they went under it.

Thales according to legend was the perfect model of the early Greek philosopher. It is said that he fell into a well while gazing at the stars, but also that he made a lot of money by cornering the market in olive-presses. There is no reason why a man who is concerned with ultimate truths should not be able to deal with the business world. Evidently Thales was equal to both.

There were severe shortcomings in the explanations offered by these philosophers, however. Each of them chose one material and made it the cause of all the others, and so we say they were monists. Unfortunately, this does not explain very much. You need to choose at least two things if you wish to make distinctions and differences, and later philosophers, as we shall soon see, did employ two. Religions, incidentally, often suffer from this lack of distinction. If you want to know the difference between a horse and a tree, it is no help to say that God made them both. The similarities do not explain as much as the differences, and you cannot have sharp differences when you have a monism. So dualisms became more the fashion in explanation.

We can look a long way back into the Greek past and see there the source in religion of the dualistic philosophies. What we now call the Greek myths were at one time of course accounts of the Greek religions. A myth is a religion in which no one any longer believes. We preserve the Greek myths because they sound so charming and quaint.

Orpheus was a Thracian god who had been taught to play the lyre by the Muses. He is also the one who went down to Hades to recover his wife, Eurydice. Our interest is not in him but in the theory of the origins of the world which was credited to him. According to one account the world was begun by two gods named Chronos (Time) and Adrasteia (Necessity)—in other words, by change and permanence. There was always to be found later in Greek philosophy a recognition of the effects of change through which threads of permanent elements were woven. To understand how change operates in the world in time, and to understand also how elements in that world do not change but to the contrary survive unchanged was a heritage that Greek philosophy bequeathed to subsequent civilizations.

A few Greek thinkers at the time did see that the world is more complicated than the early materialists had made it out, but they worked through the materials to find the complications. For Heraclitus, for instance, in the way in which fire flares up and then burns down, there is a process, and the form of that process, he declared, does not change. All things are composed of fire, and into fire they are again resolved. When he said in a famous passage that no man steps twice into the same river, he recognized both Time and Necessity, perhaps the first dualism. He brought them together under the notion of *destiny*. Everything about the river, its banks and its water, are different at different times, but the river itself remains.

He went further when he noticed that opposites like hot and cold balance each other, and so he considered the core of existence to be some kind of tension, and he gave to conflict a new importance in the nature of things. He took another step in the same direction when he looked at opposites more closely. He found that they are interdependent. Things come into existence through the conflict of opposites. In this way he concluded that all things are one.

Heraclitus had a two-story universe. There is the material world with its fire, its conflicts and opposites. But there is also the universal law which matter obeys but which is above and beyond the material. It is not supernatural or spiritual, only the result of the recognition that the regularities in nature stand out above the changes which take place in nature. In this way Heraclitus recognized the importance of the twin notions of *permanence* and *change*. The name by which the laws of nature have come to be known is the *logos*. Men are associated with it, he declared, yet they are separated from it. It is a unity, for all laws are related. And just as the *law* stood for permanence in Heraclitus' philosophy, so *fire* stood for change. Nothing changes so fast as fire.

He admired nobility of character and steadfastness of aim. We live, he said, in a world in which war is widespread and dominant. The strength of man lies in social laws, which are similar to natural laws but not as reliable. Therefore such laws are all the more to be defended. Only in sleep does a man turn to a world of his own.

The early philosophers were *materialists*, which is to say, they were looking for the causes of things in the things themselves. The causes of material things must be some kind of essential material. But they soon found that material things are not all that simple. Matter, as it was turning out, is not just a stuff, it contains principles in terms of which explanations can be made. If for instance opposition can be found in matter then opposites will have to be dealt with separately, if *up and down* are opposites, and *cold and hot,* then perhaps *earth and fire* are, too. *Opposition* itself became one of the explanatory principles, and others began to be discovered. If something could be now in one state and now in another which was its opposite, then there must be some kind of close association of opposites more important than either of them. Hence general ideas like *identity, difference* and *change* took the place of the old materials.

Not everyone agreed, of course. There were at the time philosophers who rejected the old religions but at the same time thought that the explanations offered by the materialists were too simple. Two of these thinkers were not convinced that some kind of matter was the essence of the world. One of them, Anaximander, chose a kind of neutral stuff, an indefinite something, from which pairs of opposites, such as *hot and cold* or *wet and dry,* emerged, and into which they fell back.

The second of these thinkers, the philosopher named Pythagoras, hit upon another idea about the world stuff which he thought just as general as Anaximander's "indefinite" but at the same time was more familiar. It takes a genius to point out that something which is generally known might be more important than anyone had thought, and this is exactly what Pythagoras did. *Number,* he said, is the reality of things, *all real things are numbers.* He recognized the importance of opposites, too, but for him the opposites chosen were *limits* and the *unlimited.* He could find what he wanted in arithmetic.

Unfortunately, his followers considered him a god and his ideas received a kind of religious endorsement. It was claimed that he himself wrote nothing but that he lectured in secret to a small band of followers; that he had a golden thigh; that he was a wonder worker; and that he taught among other doctrines the transmigration of souls. A curious combination of mysticism and science came out of his teachings and indeed as a consequence his followers went off in two different directions. One was mysticism, the theory that the divine can be reached without the aid of reason, but the other was science, which relies upon reason and fact.

The next great name among the early philosophers was that of Parmenides. We can understand his teaching best perhaps by comparing it with the teaching of Heraclitus. Where Heraclitus had insisted on the importance of change, Parmenides emphasized permanence. He thought that change was always a change in the parts of some whole, while the whole itself does not change, much as the parts in an engine move while the engine itself does not move in relation to the parts. How would it be, he suggested, if we were to suppose that the largest whole does not change while all of its parts do, and if we were to suppose further that the universe is that largest whole?

At this point he introduced a new pair of notions: he divided everything into *appearance* and *reality. Appearance* is how things look to us, and *reality* is how they really are. There was here of course the additional notion that how things look is not how they are, that appearances, in other words, are false. It should now be possible to see how philosophers work, that they aim at comprehensiveness. We have just seen that Parmenides had two pairs of notions: whole-and-part and appearance-and-reality. All that remained to do was to put them together. Now, he said, let us suppose that the *whole* universe is *real*, while its *parts* present a false *appearance*.

Parmenides thereby expressed the first comprehensive theory of reality of which we have any record. It is not complete but it does give us some insight into how the enterprise of philosophy got its start. This is the kind of inquiry we have come to call *metaphysics*, though at the time it had no special name. How it acquired that name I will tell you later.

Not everyone agreed with Parmenides, of course. We can imagine his opponents saying that our senses—our sight, hearing and touch for example—never tell us about the whole, only about the parts. "Are you suggesting," they pressed on, "that the evidence of our senses is false?"

His reply was earth-shaking and has seemed so to all men since then. "That is just what I am suggesting," he replied, and went on to complete the picture. We have another way of knowing which takes up the slack, he explained, we have minds which can reason. Through our powers of reasoning we can know the world as a whole in our thoughts. When thoughts contradict the senses, it is the thoughts in which we must put our trust. Thought tells us that reality is one which is The Whole of the universe, and that every part of it is false and misleading except as it contributes to that whole.

There is a flaw in Parmenides' thinking. He said there is a limit to The Whole. But a limit is also an end to the perfection of The Whole, for The Whole is that which lacks nothing, and that which lacks nothing cannot be limited. The idea of The Whole and the idea of limits seem to be contradictory.

Parmenides was the first *idealist*, just as Thales had been the first *materialist*. All philosophical words change their meaning from time to time, so that if you want to know the exact meaning of a word used in philosophy you have first to say what philosopher used it. The word *idealist* has come to mean that the reality of the world consists in our ideas about it, that *reality*, in short, is *mental*.

Parmenides received a great deal of support from other philosophers. Some of them became famous because they worked out clever defenses of his position. Zeno was particularly successful in this respect because of his arguments in defense of the theory that change is illusory. Some philosophers are famous for the breadth and sweep of their ideas, others for the importance of the problems they raised. Parmenides made a system of ideas, which to Zeno suggested the following problem. If the parts of the whole are not real, he said, then neither is change, for only the parts change, not the whole of which they are parts. And if change is not real then neither is motion, because motion is the most obvious of all the kinds of change.

Zeno gave two examples. The first concerned a man—he named the Homeric hero, Achilles—and a turtle. Everyone knows that a man can run faster than a turtle and therefore catch him, but, Zeno argued, the appearance that he can do so is false. Zeno broke up the distance between them into infinitely many parts and then showed that the man could never cover an infinite distance, but that even if he could the turtle would not be there for it would have moved even if only a little. Since no one can take an infinite number of steps in a finite length of time, Achilles could never catch the turtle. As Epicurus was later to say, the sum of things is infinite, yet there cannot be an infinite sum, for how is it possible for instance to add a column of figures when it has no end?

To show you how slowly things move in philosophy, this problem was not solved until the 19th century, after some 2400 years, and then not by a philosopher but by a mathematician. I will tell you in a little while what the solution was.

Sometimes I think the philosophers at any given period try all of the combinations that are possible with the ideas they have on hand. This was true of the Greeks certainly, and in a certain sense it has always been true. The early philosophers ran the whole range. For example, another early philosopher named Empedocles made another system of what had been left to him by the materialists. The universe, he declared, is filled with materials. Earth, air, fire and water fill all space without re-mainder. Nature consists in their mixture, but nothing comes into existence or goes out of it. Sometimes the materials pull together and sometimes they pull apart. When they pull to-gether there is harmony—love, he called it; and when they pull apart there is strife. Love and strife alternate in ruling the world.

Like so many early Greek philosophers, Pythagoras especially, Empedocles enjoyed great fame and was credited with magic powers, which he himself may or may not have claimed. We shall never know, but it was typical of the times to mix up reason and fact with supernatural gifts. Those who were able to make lucky guesses were so rare that they were held to be divine.

Democritus, the last and one of the most important of the early Greek philosophers we shall want to look at, was a little later than the others but his work somehow seems to be related to theirs.

He is said to have written sixty books but none has survived. He was famous in his own day, yet Plato, who was his con-temporary, never mentioned him. We know something of his ideas from other people, and especially from a much later Roman philosopher named Lucretius, who wrote a book-length poem after the custom of the times, retelling Democritus' ideas.

Democritus followed closely the thought of another man named Leucippus, who had the reasoning of Parmenides and the materialism of the others to go on. Their problem could be stated somewhat like this. How is it possible to deal with the idea of different materials by means of reason?

Every genius is responsible for at least one new and brilliant idea. The brilliant idea that occurred to Democritus was this. He could unite the four materials, earth, air, fire and water, by breaking up each of them and finding the same parts in all.

Mind you, he did not actually break them up; he could not, not with the little equipment he had to call on. He performed the analysis only as an act of imagination; he *supposed* them broken up into very many similar parts, which he called "atoms."

He could not mean by this word what we have come to mean by it. He meant merely something which could not be split any further. In Greek "a-tom" means "uncuttable."

So now he was ready with an explanation of nature (including man). It was composed of a great many very small pieces of matter, all of them in continual motion. Beyond them there was only empty space. The atoms themselves were capable of more combinations of atoms than there were atoms, and many worlds could come into existence and go out of existence as the atoms combined and separated again.

Just as Parmenides had been a monist in believing that reality consists in a single great whole, so Democritus was a pluralist in believing that it consists in many small parts. But his "atoms" were exceedingly small and you could not see or feel them. They had size only, and the sense qualities that we suppose them to have, the colors, sounds, tastes, odors, were actually added to them by the mind.

With his new theory Democritus still had to answer critics who counted upon the evidence of the senses. Most materialists rely very much upon sense evidence, sometimes entirely. But here was a materialist who did not. He had reached the conclusion that all was composed of atoms just by thinking about the problem.

Here he hit upon another important idea. If you think of the evidence of the senses in terms of what the senses pick up, you may note that we have always used the word "qualities."

Now what Democritus claimed was that the atoms have no qualities, only physical properties, and that the qualities which material things seem to have are contributed by the human senses. If material things have colors, make sounds and have typical odors, it is because the human sense organs put them there.

This is a purely mechanical picture of the world and as a matter of fact materialists are often mechanists. Things do what they do because it is in them to act in that way. There is no need for God as an explanation of matter, and only some of its qualities rely upon the human mind. Others, such as the physical properties, belong to it. The reality of material atoms stands in that way independent of both God and man.

Leucippus and Democritus were, like the earliest Greek philosophers, the advance agents of science. They were moving in that direction even though they did not have the necessary laboratory instruments. Greek scientists, men like Archimedes and Appolonius, for instance, did have some instruments and understood the correct scientific method, but had not learned the trick of building on each other's work. Instead, each started from the beginning, and so their findings did not accumulate in the way in which they have done since the seventeenth century.

There was something clean and refreshing about the early Greek philosophers taken all together. When we try to determine what that was, it turns out to have been just a disarming honesty, a determination to look the world straight in the face and say what they saw. What they saw when they try to describe it sounds exceedingly modern.

Consider sex, for instance. Empedocles made a charming reference to "the divided meadows of Aphrodite," to "life-giving Aphrodite," but Democritus drew back. Intercourse, he declared, "is like a slight attack of apoplexy."

Or consider death. As Democritus said, "it is unreasonable not to submit to the necessary conditions of life." For Heraclitus the "dead are nastier than dung." Epicharmus insisted that he did not want to die—"but being dead, I don't mind that."

And, finally, knowledge. Heraclitus said that "men who love wisdom must be inquirers into very many things indeed." But according to Metrodorus "None of us knows anything, not even whether we know or do not know," and so, for Xenophanes "as for certain truth, no man has seen it." However, Heraclitus assured us that "Nature loves to hide" and Democritus that "many who have not learned reason, nevertheless live in accordance with reason."

We have been examining the ideas of those Greek philosophers who lived before the high period of culture which produced Socrates, Plato and Aristotle. We have only pitifully few fragments of the work of those earlier men, and what these fragments tell us mostly is what we have lost. So much, so very much, has disappeared. If we take the whole body of what remains, however, we can see that what the Greeks left us is the alphabet of abstract thought, ideas which can be combined and recombined into meaningful assemblies, out of which the drive and direction of our own philosophies have come. This is especially true of those philosophies we are now to examine.

Chapter IV

The Greatest
Greek Philosophers

Curiosity, the drive to find answers to the most fundamental questions, is the oldest and most persistent of human interests. The answer to the question, What is it all about? is most often satisfied by religion, the fine arts or philosophy. The investigation has been chiefly conducted in three areas of inquiry: *nature*, *God* and *man*. Each has at one time or another been given a central place and the other two places of lesser importance.

For the Greeks *nature* was central, and all-inclusive, *man* second and *God* third. In the ancient Greek view both God and man are parts of nature, but man is slightly more important than God as an object of study. In later chapters we shall see that other arrangements have often been made.

In the ancient Greek view, inquiry was directed first at nature, in which man was somehow imbedded and God fixed as its cause and mover. The Greeks did not know much about nature; with only their unaided senses not much could be learned. But they worked out what they could.

We have been talking about the philosophers who flourished before 600 B.C. Now we shall consider those who lived in the best period of Greece, 600 to 400 B.C., some 2400 years ago. We have seen that the men who investigated nature sought no help from the idea of God. Other philosophers were to come who would think that a broad understanding of nature was not necessary because the understanding of God, who is different from nature, must be the first consideration. But at the height of ancient Greek civilization around 500 B.C., there appeared a group of men who were interested only in the human enterprise, and they measured it by practical success. These were the Sophists, brilliant teachers employed by the rich to instruct their sons. They took the place of the university professors, as you might have found them for instance in England in the last century at Oxford and Cambridge where only the children of aristocrats could afford an education.

Perhaps because the Sophists were Greek and so had a general turn of mind, they saw practical success in terms of a set of principles. The first of these was that man should be interested only in himself, and in nature only to the extent to which it would pay him to think about it. Man, not nature or God, is "the measure of all things," Protagoras declared. The Sophists (the word means "men of wisdom") taught their young charges how to win arguments in the law courts and not to be concerned with right or wrong. The truth is relative anyway, they said, and all that justice represents is the interest of the stronger. It is legitimate to use any means to gain an end, for the end always justifies the means.

We know this contention well. It is always used by those who brutally exploit others, and it works more often for big nations than for small. There is no arguing with the winners, for the losers lose everything, including their lives. And if in time it happens that past judgments are reversed, what difference can that make to the dead? This position is met with often enough in the practice of law and in the life of politics, and the Greeks were of course very much involved in both. For they lived a public life more intensely than a private one.

There is no doubt that for a brief while at least the Greeks enjoyed prosperity. Theirs was a small country, compared to the Persian Empire for instance, but they grew wealthy on manufacture and international trade, even if it was all on the small scale of those times. But the puzzle and the mystery was that in addition to their business triumphs they managed to produce also the beginnings of theatre, experimental science, history, poetry, sculpture and painting and architecture.

In addition they produced philosophers who challenged the gospel of practical success, just as England in the days of Empire produced men who questioned the right of Englishmen to rule over others. The first of these Greek philosophers was Socrates, the son of a stone-cutter and a midwife. He was ugly, enormously strong, and above all utterly charming as well as brilliant. He was mistaken for a Sophist at first because of his rich friends and because he was a teacher, but he took no money for his teaching, and in fact quarreled with the Sophists in public displays of argument that dazzled everyone.

His view was that success could never be more than a short-term affair unless it was founded on logical truth and moral right. He was a moral counter-puncher. That is to say, he would never declare anything first, but when he had led his opponent into stating a position he would engage him in a dialogue which ended by showing how untenable that position was. This would leave both sides nowhere, but at least with open minds and prepared to look further. "The unexamined life is not worth living" was his motto, and he invited all and sundry to examine life along with him.

A much later writer has preserved for us some anecdotes about Socrates. In the *Lives of Eminent Philosophers* Diogenes Laertius has recorded a few of the remarks and attitudes which made Socrates famous.

Once when looking at a variety of merchandise exposed for sale, Socrates was heard to observe, "How many things I can do without!" He said that he was nearest to the gods because he had the least number of wants. He declared leisure to be the most prized of possessions. He recognized only one good: knowledge, and only one evil: ignorance.

He married twice, the second time to Xanthippe, a shrew who screamed at him repeatedly and often hit him, sometimes even in public. When asked why he put up with such behavior, he said in effect, that it was good training because if you could stand her you could stand anything else that might happen to you. When someone asked him whether to marry or not, Socrates replied, "Either way you will repent it."

He expressed astonishment that sculptors should take such pains to make perfect likenesses of men in marble but not to take the same pains to perfect their own characters. He once remarked that from the trees he could learn nothing, and confined his interests chiefly to man himself.

Lurking behind the conversations of Socrates there can be detected the ultimate question of human behavior. What is the final end of man? To enrich himself while he is alive? To cultivate a strong character and the many personal virtues? Or to be so productive that he leaves the world a better place for his having lived in it? Most men would choose the first, Socrates liked the second, I myself prefer the third.

Socrates wrote nothing, but he was surrounded by leaders from all walks of life, from Xenophon, the rough military general, to Plato, the cultivated and wealthy aristocrat. Both men wrote about him and theirs are the only pictures of him that remain. They show him to have been brave and intelligent, and possessed of a great sense of humor, but with a single fixed goal in life: to lead men to the truth. The truth, he thought, could not fail to win out in the end regardless of its temporary consequences, and the truth, he also believed, would make virtue unassailable.

Unfortunately, Socrates got mixed up with the losing side in a political struggle. His enemies, led by Miletus, accused him of corrupting the youth by "making the worse cause appear the better," and they condemned him to death. He was, in a way, almost a religious figure of reason incarnate, and the world's first martyr to the truth.

Actually, those who had convicted him did not want to see him a martyr and his friends were allowed to conspire with the jailer to help him to escape. He refused, and in the *Phaedo,* in one of the most moving accounts in all literature, Plato described his last day in his cell with his friends, and the manner of his execution. He was condemned to drink hemlock, a deadly poison, and did so, discoursing all the while on philosophy while his friends stood around him and wept.

After his death the Athenians felt such remorse that they closed the schools temporarily, put Miletus to death and banished the other accusers. Then they honored Socrates with a bronze statue. Which did not of course bring him back though it did do much to spread his teaching. That was left chiefly to his pupils.

Among them was foremost of all Plato, and it is to Plato's dialogues that we owe much of our knowledge of Socrates. The strength of the man shows also in his other disciples, however, because he was many-sided, and lesser men could each take off from some one particular aspect of his character.

Two of these men were very influential, Antisthenes the Cynic and Aristippus the Cyrenaic, and in their lives as well as in their beliefs they were opposites.

Antisthenes imitated Socrates' indifference to worldly affairs and his composure in the face of pain. "I would rather go mad than experience pleasure," he declared. When asked how to become good and noble, Antisthenes advised, "Learn from those who know what faults are to be avoided." When he wanted to pronounce a curse, he said, "May the sons of your enemies live in luxury." The good life for him was an austere life, and he thought that one should need few possessions. It was a style of life he sought, one that could not be disturbed under any circumstances. What he required of a man was a strong character.

I said that Aristippus the Cyrenaic was the opposite of Antisthenes. Where Antisthenes thought that pleasure was to be avoided at all costs and saw virtue only in enduring pain, Aristippus pursued pleasure exclusively and thought it the only good. He was very outspoken. He did not mean the pleasures of the mind but those of the body, not those long-range pleasures which come from the understanding but the immediate pleasures which are found in the moment alone.

Aristippus was what we would call an original and an eccentric, but he was also a highly intelligent man. Diogenes Laertius has some amusing stories about him. Here are a few.

When asked why philosophers visit rich men but rich men no longer visit philosophers, Aristippus replied, "Because the philosophers know what they need while the rich men do not." He said, slyly, that he did not take money for his own use but to teach the givers what they should spend their money on.

One day he was seen by a disciple going into a whore house. He defended his action by saying, "It is not going in that is dangerous, but being unable to go out." When one of the girls told him she was pregnant by him, he answered, "You are no more sure of this than if you had run through some coarse weeds and could tell which one had stuck you."

Of all Socrates' many disciples, it was only Plato who was destined to exceed the master. Like so many great men, Plato was the perfect expression of the age in which he lived. Also, he was lucky. Greek civilization was at its very height. The Persian invaders had been turned back twice, in 490 B.C. and again in 480. Pericles, the greatest Athenian statesman had just died. Plato was born in 427 and lived to be eighty. His family was wealthy and he must have had considerable health. At first he tried his hand at literature but had little success. It was Socrates who turned him to philosophy, and he founded a school called the Academy, after its location in Hecademus Park. For years he wrote and taught there. He must have been very arrogant. It was said that he had wished to buy up and burn all the writings of Democritus but was dissuaded because the books had been too widely circulated. Antisthenes reported visiting him once when he was ill. Plato had been vomiting into a basin.

Antisthenes looked at it and said, "I see the bile but not the pride."

Plato had a friend who was the dictator of Syracuse, a city on the southeast coast of Sicily, and who invited him to come there to put his political and ethical ideas into practice. He tried this three times and failed three times, twice barely escaping with his life. Like so many thinkers he was a failure at practice, but the many books he left us have influenced the world ever since.

Socrates' pursuit of the truth was taken up by Plato and elaborated. What Plato discovered was that there are two worlds, not one. You may remember that there had been other divisions considered fundamental by philosophers. *Identity and difference* was a favorite, and so was *permanence and change*. But Plato made for the first time what I shall henceforth call the "grand division." He distinguished between a world of material objects in space and time corresponding to the reports of our senses, and a world of abstract ideas corresponding to our thoughts.

He could have been brought to this view by attempting to bring together the fire of Heraclitus and the logic of Parmenides, or it might have been suggested to him by the division Heraclitus had made between the world of matter and the laws governing matter which he called, if you remember, the *logos*.

But there was another development which might have suggested the division, and it is worth pausing a moment to look at. In Greece at the time there were two distinct religions. There were the sky gods which the Greeks had brought to Greece with them from wherever they came. These are the gods with which we are so familiar from our readings of Homer; the chief God, Zeus, his wife, Hera, and others, such as Apollo, Athena, Hermes, and Aphrodite. These are known as the Olympian Gods because they lived on the top of Mt. Olympus.

But the people who were already in Greece, and whom the Greeks conquered, also had their religion, made up for the most part of earth gods. Their services, celebrated in underground temples, were known as "mysteries" and their priests made prophecies. The Orphic and Eleusinian Mysteries and the Delphic Oracle were often consulted by earnest citizens and their predictions taken quite seriously. Someone asked the Pythian prophetess at Delphi who was the wisest man in Greece, and the reply was "Socrates." When this was reported to him, he reflected on it and came to the conclusion that it was because he knew what he did not know.

Since the sky gods and earth gods were quite separate they might easily have suggested to Plato the existence of two worlds, the sky gods representing the world of reason and the earth gods representing the world of matter.

There is no doubt a world of matter corresponding to our senses. But there is also another world corresponding to our thoughts about it. Plato called the first the world of "sensible things" because although they are quite independent of our senses we do learn about them through our senses. And he called the second the world of "intelligible things" because in the same way although they are quite independent of our thoughts we learn about them through our thoughts. The first is not difficult to understand, for everyone knows about the material world. But the second gives trouble, because its existence is not as easy to grasp. Let me see if I can be of any help.

Imagine, then, a world to which belong no material things but only the *classes* of material things, not Tom, Dick and Harry but *man*, not round drinking glasses and round wheels but *roundness* itself. Imagine also that the *laws* which we learn about by observing the uniform behavior of material things, the law of gravitation for instance, belong to that same abstract world. And finally imagine that such abstract objects as classes and laws are *ideal* in the sense of perfection.

These *classes*, *laws* and *ideals* are different from material things in a number of important ways. They are immaterial and they are permanent. They do not perish when material things do, but survive so far as we can tell forever. Plato's name for them was "*Ideas*," a word we now use for thoughts. We shall see that Aristotle called them "*forms*" and in the Middle Ages they came to be known as "*universals*."

Curiously, it is never material things but only their *classes* and *parts* which survive as Ideas. We have discussed the classes already, but not the parts. Let us consider that there are two kinds of parts: qualities and relations. The qualities, such as redness, hardness, sweetness, are the same in every material thing but are not themselves material; they are Platonic Ideas. The same is true of relations. Position and number, for instance, are relations which are Platonic Ideas. They can no more perish than the qualities. Values, such as goodness or beauty, are also qualities.

I know none of this is easy to understand at first and I will try to clarify it as much as I can, but you yourself will have to work at it a little. Understanding that some of the things we encounter in existence, the colors and the shapes for instance, are something special because they alone do not perish and so are not subject to time, is very difficult, but bear with me. I know it is hard to get yourself into that frame of mind where you are talking not about anything in particular but only about things in general. Philosophy is like chess, a game played with counters as though they were otherwise meaningless, but while the chessmen do not have any necessary reference to the real world, the philosophical terms do. Only, you must learn to manipulate them as though they did not.

You will find most philosophy quite impossible unless you distinguish between *belief* and *understanding*. If I say that the moon is made of green cheese, you will not believe what I say but you will understand me. So please do not make the mistake of making belief a condition for understanding, because then you could understand only one philosophy—that is, since many of them conflict, you could not possibly believe them all.

The theory of the Ideas has been both attacked and defended ever since Plato first put it forward. Chief among the arguments against it, of course, was that, unlike statements about material things which are based on the evidence of the senses, the truth about the Ideas could not be checked by others. If the world corresponds to my thoughts, it is only I who can check them. Then, too, Ideas do not represent anything very solid, like material things, so how can we believe in them more than we believe in material things?

Plato's own answer, of course, was that the Ideas are eternal while material things change and perish, and what is eternal can be believed in absolutely. A particular statement, such as "It is raining" or "We are at war now" may be true today and false tomorrow, while "2+2 = 4" is true now and forever. But if some things are eternal perhaps there is a special condition for them in which they are removed from the material world altogether. This would be true, certainly, if they were not concrete and vivid, like material things, but only abstract possibilities. For then they could be found in the material world yet not belong wholly to it.

Plato weakened his case for the reality of his Ideas by doubting the equal reality of the material things in which men have almost always believed. We shall see when we come to look at the rise of experimental science some two thousand years later that a new argument for Plato's defense of his theory of Ideas (though not of his attack on the reality of material things) has arisen. For what the scientists are after is not the knowledge of material things but of general laws governing those material things. They look at the material things themselves but only for evidence of such laws. And the laws of science resemble Plato's Ideas much more than they do material things.

Plato thought that there are *two* external worlds. He thought the shapes in the material world reflect the forms in the ideal world, and that the difference between them was one of appearance and reality. He thought, in other words, that the sensible things were pale and imperfect copies of the intelligible things, reflecting them and therefore only partly real. An intelligent man in this case would not bother to learn from his senses since they report only unreliable knowledge, knowledge of what would be here today and gone tomorrow. He would concentrate on thinking about the Ideas and about the relations between them.

Of course if the sensible things only reflected the intelligible things, then the sensible things could not be as real. The round things, the men, the beautiful things we see, are only temporary and very faint copies of "circularity," of "manhood" and of "beauty," which exist forever in the world of Ideas.

That is the way Plato wrote about them most of the time, and it is the way his theory is chiefly remembered. But there are a few other passages which credit more reality to sensible things. In one, for instance, Plato compared intelligible things with sunlight, which is everywhere as *real* when it strikes the earth as it is on the sun but is nowhere as *much*. Another illustration which might be useful is that of a slice of cake, which is not *as much* cake as the whole cake but is just as "*cakey*." In other words, according to this theory of sensible things, they participate in the reality of intelligible things rather than merely reflect them. Plato's participation theory makes sensible things as real as intelligible things even though of a different order of reality.

By doing this, however, Plato missed two obvious points. He failed to notice that the things that change do so steadily, and that rates of change do not themselves change. And he failed to notice that while sensible things perish, others very much like them take their place, so that the *forms* of those things recur. It is the forms of material things which we call "universals" when we think about them in another way. And so it is worth our while to attend to the forms of things in our sensible experience.

Plato is known chiefly for his theory of the Ideas, but he had a lot to say about many other topics. He is first in our memory perhaps because so much of the work of earlier philosophers was lost. Plato preferred a life of contemplation to one of intense sense experience. The senses he thought should be kept in a subordinate position. As to action, it should be devoted to the improvement of government and of society generally. Plato had the first theory of art, of which we have any record, even though it is not a theory with which we would now agree, and he set forth the first elaborate theory of morals.

I pointed out in the first chapter of this book that for most people today, the word "moral" has to do with those sexual practices which are not approved. Of course, it means more than that. It refers in fact to all human behavior and even beyond. The theory of what is good and bad and what is *right* and *wrong* in morality is called *ethics*. Since Plato's writings on ethics have been so influential over the centuries, I will have to say a few words about them.

The chief point of Plato's ethics is contained, as we should expect, in his theory of the good. He spent a great deal of time pointing out first what the good is not. It is not sensual pleasures; they do not last long enough to make them worthy of our dedication. Plato compared sensual pleasures to the pleasures of scratching an itch: it has to be done again and again, and the pleasure of doing it runs out.

Instead he recommended the pleasures of the intellectual life. The good consists in the contemplation of the Ideas. Knowledge gained through abstract thought is not apt to let us down, and remains a pleasure forever because its object is eternal. Sensual pleasures may be retained but always as something less than intellectual pleasures. Plato did not want the pleasures of the moment to interfere with the pursuit of those pleasures which would be best in the long run. The test of goodness is to accord everything its just due, and by practicing the principle of proportionality to employ reason as the final judge.

It must be admitted that Plato's ethics is not for everyone except as an ideal at which to aim. The moral life he was recommending was more for the philosopher, who was expected to live up to it, than for the average man, who could hope only to imitate its virtues.

Plato's ethics was directed to the individual; his social theory was treated largely in a work on politics, the famous *Republic*, which has been described by some as the greatest book ever written. In the *Republic* Plato touched on many other topics, such as his theory of the Ideas and his theory of knowledge, but it is the politics with which we will be chiefly concerned here.

The whole work is presented as an essay on justice. It is an outline—the first we have—of the ideal state. Plato professed to find justice difficult to define, and sought to discover it through a discussion of what constitutes the political ideal. Plato had in mind of course a small city-state, possibly such as Athens was at the time, but it has been pointed out that he probably had Sparta in mind.

The state has its origins in the wants of man and so has an economic basis. There is a division of labor, based on the special talents of the individual. Its citizens are to be divided into three distinct classes. First are the Guardians or rulers, next the Auxiliaries or military class, and last the Artisans or workers. There are to be slaves, too, as there were in all of the Greek city-states at the time. Citizens are to be trained from birth in music and gymnastics. The strongest and most intelligent of the Artisan class will be chosen to be Auxiliaries, and from the Auxiliaries those who are the most patriotic, intelligent and courageous will be selected as Guardians. These will be trained in mathematics, astronomy and harmonics. By the time the prospective Guardians are thirty years of age, they are ready to be schooled in philosophy for the next five years. From the ages of thirty-five to fifty they will govern the state as philosopher-kings, after which they will be allowed to retire to a life of philosophical contemplation unless needed again to govern.

In the fifth Book of the *Republic* Plato made some proposals concerning the education of the citizens. He suggested that women should be considered the equals of men and share the work of men, including war, and they could be educated as men were. The Artisan class, numerically the largest by far, would retain private property and continue the institution of the family, but for the upper two classes both private property and family life would be abolished for the good of the state. Marriages would be arranged by lot for all Guardians and Auxiliaries, that is to say, for the rulers and the military, and they would be allowed to have only a prescribed number of children and these only at prescribed times. Children who proved to be not suited to their high station would be demoted to the class of Artisans or workers.

The *Republic* from our point of view is a strange mixture of radical ideas and very conservative ones. The equality of men and women was a theory not put into practice until comparatively recent times, and women soldiers still are not sent into battle. On the conservative side Plato ruled out poets from his ideal city-state on the grounds that their work was too disturbing. Hesiod and Homer told disgraceful tales of the doings of the gods, and so would not be furnishing good examples of behavior. Only men between the ages of twenty-five and fifty-five would be allowed to beget children, and only women between twenty and forty would be allowed to bear them.

For the first time perhaps (and despite Plato's own failure in Syracuse) the rulers were to be philosophers. They would have to know what is true and good if they were to arrange the life of the state.

Plato admitted that to move from the existing city-state to the one he considered ideal, to put, in other words, his ideal into practice, would prove difficult. The smallest change that might practically be made in the attempt to achieve the ideal would be to make the philosopher a king. Plato's objection to democracy was that politicians rather than statesmen would rule, as though no special knowledge was required of the ruler.

And so now we can see at the end of the *Republic* just what justice was in Plato's view. Unable to define justice as such, he led us to see its definition through the outlines of the perfect state. Justice is due proportionality: rendering to each individual what is due him and to each class what is proper to it. It was to be achieved by each individual attending to his own business and not interfering with the business of others.

Plato has been accused of having invented the fascist state because of the element of totalitarian control in his description. He intended of course no such thing. He was looking for balance and perfection, and hoped for a structure in which each individual could do what it is best for him to do. There were drawbacks, however. Plato envisaged a world of city-states, such as indeed Greece was at the time, and he made no provision for their getting together.

Nor did he make provision for the government of the large populations, which, he must have known, existed at the time in such countries as Persia. After all they hardly counted since they were not Greek. Worst of all perhaps is the fact that he made no provision in his city-state for the production of men like himself. There was evidently never to be another Plato.

Plato was the greatest philosopher in history, and not so much for his ideas, though he had many important ones, as for the problems he suggested. Collectively the Greeks made a kind of dictionary of the theories which are possible in philosophy, so that later thinkers could make new choices of them and find fresh combinations among them. The biggest contributor was Plato. And so we have all been Platonists to some extent, as the English-American philosopher, Whitehead, was so fond of pointing out.

Plato must have been an excellent teacher, because he had as a student for twenty years a young man named Aristotle, who later became as famous as Plato was and accomplished almost as much. Aristotle studied with Plato for twenty years but left the Academy when Plato was still alive. When Aristotle departed, Plato is said to have remarked, "Aristotle spurns me, as colts kick at the mother who bore them." When Aristotle finally set up in business on his own, it was to oppose the teachings of his master. Aristotle founded a school called the "Lyceum," because it was in a Park dedicated to the God Apollo under his title "Apollo Lyceus."

Aristotle had expected to inherit Plato's Academy, which went instead to Plato's nephew, Speusippus, but he did inherit Plato's ideas, with one large and important exception. The disputed area, as we shall see, was the theory of Ideas. Plato was what we might call a conservative dreamer. He spent more time in thinking about how things *ought to be* than he did in observing how they *are*. Aristotle got his ideas from Plato but gave them a more practical turn. His dreaming was less imaginative but his observations were sharper.

North of Greece there was a country called Macedonia. The King of Macedon whose name was Philip conquered all of Greece and made of it a subject country. He hired Aristotle to serve as a tutor to his son, Alexander. When Alexander was twenty-two years old Philip died. Philip's last plan had been to conquer Asia, and Alexander went ahead with the plan. As the English historian Tarn observed, it had never occurred to him not to. Whitehead remarked once that Alexander was a successful conqueror because he had had the right teacher!

Unlike Plato, Aristotle had an intense interest in the sensible world. He liked to examine things for himself. He dissected fishes, for instance. And when his ex-pupil Alexander was busy with the conquest of Asia, he sent botanical and biological specimens, all the strange plants and animals he could find, in fact, back to Aristotle in Athens.

Aristotle did in philosophy just what students often feel in the end that they have to do in order to stand on their own feet. He rejected the philosophy of his master Plato. Had Plato said that there was a separate world of Ideas? Then Aristotle declared there was not. Had Plato said that material things were not real? Then Aristotle declared that they are as real as the Ideas because they contain the Ideas.

Aristotle was a materialist, but materialism comes in many shapes and sizes. You can be the kind of materialist who thinks that reality is exclusively confined to material things and that classes simply do not exist except as descriptions of groups of similar material things. If you say for instance of a group of red things that they are red, it does not mean that redness exists, it only means that there are things which have their redness in common. But Aristotle was not this kind of limited materialist. He thought that he had better find some place for Plato's Ideas even if they were not to have their own separate world.

So he declared that forms exist *in* things, and in this way rejected the distinction between appearance and reality. What appears is the material world together with its qualities and relations, in a word, its forms. The form of an individual, he said, is its universal, and every individual has a form. There is no such thing as formless matter, he admitted; but he insisted that there was no such thing, either, as matterless form. He accused Plato of supposing that there is a world of forms apart from matter, a situation which he found indefensible.

And so, using the same ideas Plato had used, he made a simpler arrangement. He put the intelligible things exclusively in the world of matter, in other words he put the forms in the sensible things. In that way there need be only the world that we know so familiarly, the world of material things which was now also a world containing forms.

But the very simplicity could be misleading, when the world he was trying in this way to describe was not itself necessarily all that simple. For instance, how can the universal exist in the individual? Perhaps the difficulty will be seen better if I put it in terms of classes. A class, you will recall, is a group of things, called members, having a common property. In the sense of a universal, the classes referred to are those with an unlimited number of members. Circle, for example, or planet. Universals are the same as classes, and individuals are the same as members of classes. Now ask yourself, *how can the class itself exist completely in each individual?* How, for example, can the class *tree* exist in the oak in my front yard? For that is what Aristotle expected us to suppose.

What Aristotle accomplished was to enrich our notions about the world of matter. He was able to do this by taking seriously the evidence of our senses, and taking it much more seriously than Plato had ever done. If we know that there are particular material things, such as chairs, oranges, and people, it is because we can see, hear, touch, smell or taste them. But what we experience are objects having forms. Chairs, oranges and people each have their own forms. Aristotle not only said that matter contains forms which are essentially universal, but he went much further. He was interested in motion in a way in which Plato had not been. All matter is in a constant state of motion, and if motion is that common then an explanation of motion must be found. Once again Aristotle looked deeply into the world of matter for an answer, for he did not want to go outside it.

What he found was an order in which motions succeed one another. The cause of motion is a kind of motion, a motion that causes other motions. If a present motion was caused by the motion which occurred immediately before it, and that one in turn was caused by a preceding one, then motion itself could be said to have been caused by a first mover. More than that he could not say, since we know little about the first mover, except that it itself does not move. He called it an *unmoved mover.*

From that position his thinking could go in one of two ways, and he tried both of them. The first way was to look for other causes of the condition in which we find each separate piece of matter. The second way was to guess about the condition of the first mover itself.

The change in any material thing, he said accordingly, has not one cause but four. It has a *material cause,* which is to say, some kind of substance or stuff. It has something which moves it, its *efficient cause* was his name for it. There is something which it is moved *toward,* or its *formal cause,* and something which it is moved *for,* or its *final cause.*

As an example let us consider a painter who is making a portrait. The material cause, Aristotle would say, is the paint, the canvas, the easel, the brushes, all the materials which are used in its making. The painter himself is the efficient cause. A likeness of the sitter, which is what the painter aims at, would be the formal cause. And the completed portrait would be the final cause.

I have chosen an example which is easy to describe. But I can think of many material things of which this would not be true. I claim to know what the final cause of a man is; for me it is the service of society. But what is the final cause of an antelope or a planet?

Because of this and other difficulties the only two causes of motion of Aristotle's which have survived in any important way are the material and the formal causes. We can say what the materials of an antelope and a planet consist in, and what the forms are like, but we don't know why there are antelopes and planets.

For Plato the world of matter had been created, but not so for Aristotle. He said that the world has always been here, and that only its motion was caused. God plays a larger part in Aristotle's philosophy than in Plato's, however, despite the fact that Aristotle's God is remote and preoccupied. Aristotle's God is not concerned with man; in fact, it is the other way around: man is concerned with God. The effect of a God is like that of a huge magnet which causes man to move toward Him. God moves the world by being the object of its aim, and so the world moves toward God. God's activity lies in thinking His own thoughts. Therefore the only God-like behavior open to man is to think like God, and God's thinking is about universals, not about individuals; it is pure abstract thought. God is eternally perfect, and as he is always so we would like to be sometimes. "On such a principle depends the heavens and the world of nature." Note that Aristotle said "on such a principle," not "on such a person." God is "a living being, eternal, and most good," though certainly not a great big beautiful animal as we imagine a perfect man might be.

Both Plato and Aristotle have been called "realists" because in both their philosophies reality lies outside the mind. For both of them the reality which is inside the mind came there from the outside. Thus it is possible to think of them in the same way, though with this important difference: Outside Plato's mind he thought there were two distinct external worlds, the world of sensible things (the material world) and the world of intelligible things (the Ideas). Aristotle thought that there was only one external world, but it was a material world which at the same time contained the Ideas (or as he preferred to call them, the forms or universals).

I might pause here to answer a question which must puzzle many people nowadays. There are many attempts to explain the workings of the mind in Greek and European philosophy, but not to the exclusion of an interest in the world of matter or of an interest in society. The Asian admonition to "live within" is one which rejects society and the material world together. Eastern philosophies are for the most part mental and other-worldly. We have come too far and obtained too many rewards for that to suit us now. We are committed to live in the world and not merely in ourselves. Western society is outward bound.

The differences between the philosophies of Plato and Aristotle are important enough to justify repeating. I suppose that the differences are not as sharp as the similarities. Plato had two external worlds; one a world of material individuals, the other a world of abstract universals, and he held that the world of universals is more real. Aristotle tried to get by with only one external world, and although he too believed in universals, he thought they belonged with individuals in the material world.

The point is important and not easily grasped. Philosophy, however simply presented, is not simple and takes some working over. Try rereading the passages you have trouble with. Sometimes they clear up after a while. Try thinking of some examples of your own.

Aristotle not only enriched our notions about the world of matter, he did much to help us in our thinking—through his logic, most of which is as true and useful today as it was when he wrote it.

Aristotle's logic begins with his theory of definition. If you wish to understand any kind of reasoning you must first define the terms to be used. Aristotle defined definition itself by means of the distinction between *genus* (or class) and difference. What is the class to which the term to be defined belonged and how does it differ from other members of that class? Answer those two questions and you have your definition. Let me give an example. Suppose the word to be defined is "chair." First we find the class. Now the class to which "chair" belongs is "furniture." So we say

Chair is that kind of furniture which . . . .

To find the rest of that sentence, we have to know how "chair" differs from other members of the class "furniture." The best way to find this out is to look for what chairs do or what is done with them, what they are *for*. Chairs are made to be sat on, and no other kind of furniture is. So then we have our definition:

Chair is that kind of furniture which is used for sitting.

After words are defined, the next task is to combine them into declarative sentences. We use sentences beginning with "all" for universal sentences and "some" for particular sentences, for instance "All men are mortal" and "Some Athenians are men."

Now let us combine the sentences.

   (If) all men are mortal,
(and if) Some Athenians are men
  (then) Some Athenians are mortal

If we cancel the word which is common to the first two sentences, namely, "men," then we can see how the conclusion which is stated in the third sentence is reached.

There is more to it than that, of course, but I will leave it here as a mere suggestion of what Aristotle accomplished. The remarkable thing is how his logic has stood up all of these years. Only toward the end of the last century were men able to improve on it by widening it considerably. But it is still essentially correct.

If I have made both the definition and the argument seem simple, remember that they are often exceedingly complicated and easily deceptive, and that is why a more intense study of them is advisable, although this book is not the place for such a study.

Let me illustrate the difficulty by two amusing examples.

First the example of a definition. You know the name of the curved Australian throwing-stick, the boomerang. A friend of mine defined it this way. "A boomerang is a weapon that if you throw it and it doesn't come back, it wasn't a boomerang."

Next the example of an argument. Let us take the one given above

All men are mortal,
Some Athenians are men,
Some Athenians are mortal.

That would seem to be drawing a true conclusion from true premises. But now let us consider the same argument where the premises are false.

All gods are mortal,
Some Athenians are gods,
Some Athenians are mortal.

Here the first two sentences are plainly false, yet we are still able to draw a true conclusion from them. The reason is of course that the conclusion depends upon the *form* of the argument and not upon the truth of the premises.

Plato did not set forth the rules of logic in the way in which Aristotle did, but of course he operated in terms of them. Someone once said that there is very little in Aristotle's thought that was not first in Plato's. But Plato presented his work in the form of dramatic dialogues, and in them he wanders from topic to topic. Aristotle had a different method of presentation. He wrote a separate treatise on each topic. For instance Plato had a theory of the good, and you will find it scattered throughout a number of his dialogues, though not exclusively in any. But Aristotle wrote several treatises on ethics and they contain little else. All great philosophers have systems and often you can see that in their work even when they did not present it in that way. Aristotle was the first thinker we know of to try to show the systematic and orderly nature of his ideas.

The good for man, according to Aristotle, is happiness, which he defined as "the rationally organized activity of the whole man," or, in other words, as the perfect functioning of the entire human being. Everything in its place, and everything in moderation; nothing too much. Aristotle was the author of the "Golden

Mean," of which we have heard so often. For example, *courage* is the mean between *cowardice* and *rashness*. *Temperance* is the mean between *total insensibility* and *utter sensuality*. *Liberality* is the mean between *stinginess* and *prodigality*.

There are serious criticisms to be made of the Golden Mean. For example, is it possible to have too much virtue, too much sympathy, too much knowledge? Aristotle, someone has pointed out, wrote all of his books in about twelve years. He must have overdone work, for a while, anyway.

I knew a man who tried to live the Golden Mean. He was an absolute monster of averages. He wanted to play one game of tennis every day, one rubber of bridge every night, have one Scotch and soda, and so on. It must have made for a very monotonous life. And it entirely left out the essential ingredient of novelty and surprise. But as a rough rule-of-thumb the Golden Mean has proved useful.

If the good consists in moderation and reason, then evil is not a religious idea but an error. Those who do evil, according to the Greeks, make a mistake, they miss the mark of virtue. Besides cautioning moderation, Aristotle agreed with Plato in thinking the intellectual life to be the highest form of life. Everyone can imitate this virtue even if no one can attain it. The result was a society that thought highly of philosophy, just as Europeans do still today.

Aristotle's theory of politics could not have been written without Plato's, though Aristotle's contribution is that he tends to see things more at ground level. Aristotle did not agree with all of Plato's political ideas. For instance he did not agree that the children of the Guardians should be raised by the state or that the Guardians should be deprived of the right to hold property.

States come into existence, Aristotle thought, when families, which exist to supply basic needs, combine to constitute a state, which exists for the sake of the good life. The state is not an artificial creation, therefore, but "a creature of nature" just as "man is by nature a political animal." The Greek love of social life was expressed in an extreme way by Aristotle: "He who is unable to live in society, or who has no need because he is sufficient for himself, must be either a beast or a god." You really should read Aristotle.

The test of a good state for Aristotle was whether it served the common interest in accordance with strict principles of justice. The family owes its existence to the need for sex and for the acquisition of property. Those who admire Aristotle's ideas —and who could not?—are embarrassed by the fact that he believed that some men are born to be slaves as others are born to be free. It was characteristic of the times of course that slavery was endorsed as legitimate. Aristotle thought that there should be a rotation of responsible citizens in positions of authority, combined with the greatest degree of flexibility and the division of labor.

Like his master Plato, Aristotle had many other fields of interest, among them psychology, astronomy, and the arts.

Aristotle's theory of art differed sharply from Plato's. If Plato had not had a very high opinion of art, it was chiefly because he had not thought well of material things. Material things are only pale copies of their Ideas, and so works of art, being only pale copies of material things, are twice removed from reality. No one who adopted Plato's view of art would ever have painted a picture or carved a statue. But Aristotle rejected this view. Art for him is real, as real as what it represents. Art, he said, discloses the universal that lies hidden in every individual, it brings out the ideal in every material thing.

The art in which he was most interested was that of the theatre. He had too strict a view of plays, though, for he held that there are rigid requirements for the six parts of every tragedy: plot, characters, diction, thought, spectacle and melody. The most important of the six is plot, which is "the end and purpose of the tragedy; and the end is everywhere the chief thing." Tragedies are about people "better than ourselves," about kings and their families, but comedies are about people "worse than ourselves," people from a lowly station in life.

The part of his theory of art which has had the strongest appeal is what he had to say about the effect of tragedy on the audience. The experience of living through a tragedy by sympathizing with the characters is an emotional one. The spectator of a good tragedy experiences a purgation of his emotions, and comes away feeling exhausted but cleaner and so better than he had felt before.

Looking back on the philosophies of Plato and Aristotle, who were not only the greatest of the Greek philosophers but the greatest philosophers of all times, we can see an important resemblance. Both had the highest ambition: they tried to construct systems of ideas more general than any other, metaphysical systems large enough to be all-inclusive. They differed on many minor points and even on some major ones, but not on the size of the problem.

It was a problem that recently has somehow got lost. It would help us, I think, to know how all of our interests fit together. We live whole lives, not fragmentary ones, and everything that we do, all of our needs and ambitions, every one of our efforts and projects, are parts of some integrated plan which in some way is hidden from us. It is the business of philosophy to bring this plan to light. The philosopher, in other words, is a student of the entire civilization in which we are so immersed that most of the time we fail to remember its existence. We miss in this way a big chance to enrich our lives.

The second way in which the philosophies of Plato and Aristotle had an important resemblance is that neither man was absolutely sure of his own position. Both proceeded gropingly, exploring their ground and making proposals which they themselves would not have been surprised to see wrong. It was not until modern times that philosophers have talked again so tentatively. If you find a man making the claim of absolute truth for all that he says and then you catch him out on some one thing, it makes you suspect the truth of whatever else he says. This is the trouble with many of the great philosophers, with Hegel for instance. But it was not the trouble with Plato and Aristotle.

Chapter V

The Decline of
Greek Philosophy

Ordinarily, when we use the word "culture" we mean chiefly the fine arts, and perhaps we include personal manners, such as table manners. (One of my friends wants to include what he calls "traffic manners," such as not cutting in ahead of a lady driver.) But we ought to mean more than the arts, we ought to mean everything that men do and make together, not only the fine arts but the sciences as well, and not only table manners but also languages, government and industry, beliefs, customs and social institutions. Also philosophy.

Cultures, both the comparatively small ones like Greece, and civilizations, including the large ones like the Roman Empire, have a shape, a life cycle, a common set of values and a single all-comprehensive viewpoint. It is the last two which allow us to regard culture as philosophy in action. Philosophy is the theory, culture the practice.

The last thing perhaps that we will ever succeed in explaining is why cultures and civilizations rise and fall. When they do so, it is all of a piece. The greatest years of Athens in philosophy were also her greatest in terms of economic power, political influence, and artistic production. All seem to be different kinds of expression of the same energy. All go together, I should say, because of beliefs in common, beliefs leading to common thoughts, feelings and actions.

In the short history of Greek flourishing the Greek city-state defeated the invading Persians on sea and on land, and fought disastrous wars with each other, two wars between Athens and Sparta, one between Sparta and Thebes, for instance, before succumbing to the control of Philip of Macedon. These wars were interruptions in a successful trading empire and in the production of works in architecture, painting, sculpture, music, drama and philosophy, as great as any the world has ever seen.

There has never been a great civilization that was not strong in terms of wealth and political power. Every culture which has produced great arts has also been rich and strong. Of course it *is* possible to have wealth and political power without producing much in the arts. This evidently was true of ancient Assyria, for instance. But not the other way round. There has hardly ever been a country which produced great arts that did *not* have great power. The one seems to be a necessary requirement of the other.

The centuries of classic Greek art were also those of great power in economic and political spheres. They were as it happens also the greatest centuries so far as Greek philosophy was concerned, the centuries which produced Plato and Aristotle. This period, roughly from the fifth through the fourth centuries B.C., has come to be known as The Golden Age of Greece.

Economic and political power on the one hand and cultural superiority and productivity on the other are usually interdependent.

Herodotus, for his great history, received a public award of ten talents (about $14,000), perhaps because he had demonstrated that all of Greece owed its freedom from the Persians to Athenian leadership.

The Golden Age was succeeded by another, which was a pale reflection of it, the so-called Silver Age. Greek civilization was followed by Hellenistic civilization, which was very much like the Greek though without the power. When Greece declined in importance, so did Greek philosophy. After a long series of hostilities, Philip defeated the Greek armies in a final battle which took place at Chaeronea in 338 B.C. and that was the end of Athenian independence. After Philip of Macedon conquered Greece and made it a Macedonian colony, Greek philosophy began to shrink in its range and interests. The Greeks had always been a very social people. Their life was conducted almost altogether in public, never at home. They thought highly of politics, and their political leaders were for the most part educated men. But the Hellenistic philosophers were not interested in social matters.

After Alexander died his generals divided up the empire he had conquered, and Greece passed over to the control of one of his generals. Later, Rome gained the ascendancy, and Greece became a small and unimportant part of the Roman Empire. Greece was reduced to the position of a cultivated province where the sons of rich Romans went to study or to find tutors who could teach them the Greek language, which every well-to-do Roman wanted to know so that he could read and imitate Greek literature, Greek history, Greek theatre, Greek philosophy.

In Athens the graduate schools founded by Plato and Aristotle continued to operate for almost a thousand years and went on producing original philosophy though of a somewhat inferior order. For obvious reasons political and social philosophy no longer interested the Greeks. They were not the masters of their political fate and so they were reduced to an interest only in their own private lives. But because they were Greek and intelligent they still thought in general terms. The result was a set of personal philosophies, some of which have become very important indeed.

Suppose that you had an inquisitive turn of mind, and that you wanted to know about fundamental things but in a very intimate way. The old topics would still be with you, but there would be changes. You would still be asking the same questions that the older philosophers had asked in happier times. The earlier philosophers had agreed that the human being has only three capacities: for *thought, feeling* and *action*. But they had put *thought* above the others. *Thought* was given a considerable preference over *feeling*, and as for *action*, it was held to be unworthy of the highest goals. Therefore the prime questions were: what should we think, rather than what should we feel or what should we do?

Plato was a philosopher first and a member of society second, and so his answers for the individual were always such as he supposed would benefit society. After the death of Aristotle and the loss of independence of the Greek city-states, the philosophers took a different attitude. The choices of the three capacities of man and how they were to be exercised became a purely personal affair. *Activity*, which had counted for so little with Plato, and only for a little more with Aristotle, was now given the place of honor in the list, with *feeling* a close second. Accordingly two groups of philosophers put *feeling* and *action* first, and when the third group chose *thought* it was of a purely negative kind.

In the philosophies of the men who arose in this period of the decline of Athens, ethics took first place over the theory of reality. Not "What is the nature of reality?" but rather "What should I do in order to lead the good life?" was their question. As we have noted, the quest for reality took place in purely personal terms. The search for the good in individual human behavior seemed to them much more important somehow than the broader question of what there is in the world. They did not try to compose a system of ideas more inclusive than any other, as for instance Plato and Aristotle had done. Instead they sought a guide to action.

The man who chose feeling as his guide was named Epicurus. Quite naturally, he preferred good feelings to bad ones, pleasure to pain. Happiness, the goal of man, consists, he thought, in the greatest amount of pleasure in the long run. That eliminated sensual pleasures, which do not last. But he defined pleasure negatively, for he said it was the absence of pain. There is so much pain in the world that to get rid of it is a positive pleasure.

What man should strive for, therefore, is *ataraxia*, a word meaning serenity, peace of mind as well as of body. The greatest and longest-lasting pleasure would be a state of repose, of utter tranquillity. He should not engage in political life—Epicurus specially warned against this—and he should not seek worldly success, neither wealth nor prestige. He should seek, in other words, throughout his life and not merely toward the end of it, for quiet retirement, away from the cares of the world.

A retreat is very far from what Epicurus' name has come to stand for. Epicureanism has passed into the language as a symbol for sensuality, a riotous life conducted almost entirely in terms of luxury in food, alcohol and sex: exquisite surroundings, great dishes, rare wines and, last but not least, beautiful women.

That is not what Epicurus had in mind. He wanted nothing so disturbing. He even cautioned against established religions, which he said are unsettling because of the terrors they inspire. Death is a sleep, and the horrors of death are experienced only by the living when they anticipate it for themselves.

One of the troubles with the kind of Epicureanism that Epicurus recommended was its economic cost. Few can afford the kind of sheltered life that is capable of bringing complete serenity with it. Mankind can be loved without interruption or disturbance of any kind only from a distance, the kind of distance a private income and a walled estate can provide.

Epicurus died at the age of 72 of a combination of strangury and dysentery, both extremely painful. During the progress of these ailments and near his own end he wrote a letter to a friend on what he described as "this blissful day." When he knew he was about to die he got into a tub of warm water with a bottle of wine. In his will he was careful to provide for his most intimate disciples and, as was the custom, freed his favorite slaves. He died as he had lived, a gentle creature of good instincts.

One of the most exciting things about the human species is the range of its interests. Somewhere and at some time, everything edible has either been eaten or prohibited, and for religious reasons. Everything has been done or else forbidden in ritual fashion. Similarly with theory, everything has been believed—or doubted. Men seem much more concerned to explore the possibilities involved in being human than to settle on any one pattern of life.

If Epicurus had advised a state of serenity based on the pursuit of happiness, his opposite number, Zeno, recommended happiness also. Only, happiness for Zeno lay in refraining from feeling. Not a feeling of serenity, just no feeling at all. This he called *apathy*, and proclaimed it to be its own end and its own reward. The Stoic did not distinguish between pleasure and pain since he tried to preserve an attitude of indifference to both. He accepted passively whatever happened, and no more elected to enjoy than to suffer.

Zeno, the founder of the Stoic school of philosophy, named after the Stoa or Painted Porch where he lectured, emigrated to Athens from his native island of Cyprus, shortly after the Macedonian general, Antipater, had put down an Athenian revolt to regain its independence. Zeno was there presumably when Antipater's successors fought for four years over the possession of Greece, but he was not new to violence. The story was told that he had been shipwrecked on a voyage from Phoenicia to Peiraeus, the port of Athens, with "a cargo of purple." Once in Athens he made for a bookshop where he first encountered Xenophon's account of Socrates and was so taken with it that he decided to become a philosopher.

It was not a happy time for philosophy or for the participation in social life. Zeno's views certainly reflected this. Virtue, he declared, lies in *in*sensibility, in austerity. The human condition is a bad one under any circumstances, therefore the less one has to do with the world, the better. There are no degrees of virtue, the withdrawal is absolute. What one does have to do is one's duty, strictly that and no more. Concede to the world only what you have to in order to discharge your social obligations.

As for events themselves, he continued, the Stoic should maintain an attitude of complete indifference to them. Good or bad luck should be received in exactly the same way. In fact, bad luck had perhaps an advantage, since it gave the Stoic an opportunity to exercise virtue. Events counted only to the extent to which they could serve individual human morality.

Clever observers have noted a family resemblance between the Epicureans and the Stoics. They appeared in about the same period of the decline of Greek civilization. Both their philosophies were built upon personal and individual considerations. Both were more concerned with rules of conduct than with theories of reality. Both borrowed their theories of reality from older, already established systems. Both were intensely negative; they were more interested in what not to do than in what to do. Both were more limited in their views than previous philosophers had been.

One chief difference was the extent of their influence. The Stoic school continued longer and because of its longer history made more changes, more concessions to the practical demands of life. Not private wisdom but temperance in human relations, not mere austerity but an obligation to carry out one's daily duties, even when they were of a public nature. The Stoic philosophy influenced the Roman leaders, many of whom professed themselves Stoics. And it influenced Christianity at its formation, turning it in the direction of asceticism and austerity. The Roman emperor and general, Marcus Aurelius, who wrote a volume of *Meditations* in his camp at night when on military campaigns, was a self-confessed Stoic of the purest kind.

The Epicureans and Stoics had a smaller number of beliefs than the great philosophers who went before them. They got along with as few principles as possible. At about the same period, however, there arose a philosopher who questioned whether one could have any principles at all. Pyrrho, the founder of the Skeptic school, had only one principle, and it was to the effect that there were no principles in which one could believe. The senses cannot be trusted, he asserted, because they are so intensely personal that they report different things to different people. As for reason, it cannot be trusted either, because it is possible to balance any statement with its opposite.

The only possible conclusion is that there must be a complete suspension of judgment. Doubt, then, remains the only reasonable belief left to the Skeptics. It is possible to doubt everything of a fundamental nature. This meant for them of course that there could be no truth and no morality. A statement is no more true than its contradictory; and since this holds also for material things their true nature cannot ever be known. The only sound belief according to the Skeptics is the statement that one cannot have any sound beliefs. The knowledge of anything absolute is absolutely unobtainable.

Something of the Stoic attitude toward the world hung over the Skeptics. Take action, for instance. In the absence of beliefs the Stoic could not see any more reason for one kind of behavior than for another. Pyrrho, so the account goes, would not go out of his way for anything, he would take no precautions but faced all risks just as they came, meeting carts, precipices or dogs in the same way; he was kept out of harm only by friends who followed close after him.

If belief is a guide to action, then Pyrrho was no help. Nevertheless he was a success in the terms of his day. He had begun life as a poor painter but before he had done he was honored by his native city of Elis who because of him declared all philosophers to be exempt from taxes.

Like all of the Greek philosophers, Pyrrho was more subtle than is ordinarily supposed. When his sister was done an injury he became enraged, and he defended this violation of his indifference by saying that it was not over a weak woman that one should display indifference. On the other hand, when he was frightened at the attack of a mad dog, he admitted that it was not easy to strip oneself of human frailty. Strive against facts, he advised, by deeds but if that was not possible then by words.

The story is told that Pyrrho was walking one day in the direction of a cliff from which he would have fallen to his death on the rocks below. A favorite student turned him aside. But it has been asked whether that student did not betray Pyrrho's Skepticism, for if the student had been a true believer he too would not have seen any more reason to take one direction than another. In short he could only have been a follower of Pyrrho's by not saving Pyrrho. In saving him he showed that he preferred the man to his beliefs.

The story illustrates the impossibility of Skepticism as a working philosophy. Pyrrho himself recognized this, for when the question arose as to how the Skeptic was to guide his actions, Pyrrho advised following custom and tradition, and for the rest employing probabilities. This is in fact just what we do a lot more times than we like to admit. If we must suspend judgment, as Pyrrho recommended, we can still act on what we estimate to be the probable consequences.

There are as a matter of fact no certainties in human life. If I plan to walk across the street, there is no guarantee that I will get there. I could have a sudden heart attack without warning or I could be hit by a truck I had not seen. Both events happen every day. But they do not happen to everyone, and in fact they happen only to a minority of people. The chances are therefore that I will cross the street safely, as indeed I have done already hundreds of times.

We use probability as a guide to life without ever thinking about it. If my chance of getting safely across the street is a pretty good one, then I start over, even though no one can guarantee success and some do not make it. We do everything that we do in much that same way. No one can give us a positive assurance that we will live to complete the programs we adopt, whether they are short or long. We take our chances simply because the odds are favorable, not because the outcome is certain. Life itself is uncertain, but that does not prevent us from living it to the utmost of which we are capable.

Pyrrhonism, or Skepticism, is not a complete philosophy, yet it has a legitimate place as part of everyone's procedure. If we were to doubt everything of which we have reason to doubt, we might arrive at a better collection of beliefs. For it is the beliefs which have demonstrated that they can withstand doubt, not those we have never doubted, which are entitled to carry the seal of evidence. The intelligent man questions everything, and believes only what there is sufficient evidence for believing.

The main difficulty with all three of these late Greek philosophers, the Epicureans, the Stoics and the Skeptics, is that their philosophies fall short somehow both as guides to life and as explanations of existence.

As guides to life each of the three philosophies fails because each recommends only one kind of behavior. The individual has a variety of encounters with the world, he finds himself in all sorts of situations and is confronted with many sorts of problems, many sorts of people. How is he to deal with them? Surely not always in the same way. I have found for instance that people respond to that side of me which they encounter, and I have many sides to my character and personality, as everyone has. I do not think it is necessary to go quite so far as Will Rogers, the American comedian, when he said that he had never met a man he did not like. Yet it is true that the more people you know, the richer your life is. People are not all on the same wavelength. Should anyone be guided through life by a single attitude and a simple formula? I hope not. We need to be as complex as necessary in order to make the various responses which are required by different challenges, and every personality is a fresh challenge.

As explanations of existence each of the three philosophies fails for a similar reason. In their accounts the world seems too simple. The world beyond the individual contains many more aspects than you would ever know from their descriptions. One explanation for everything is not enough. While it is true that the Epicureans and Stoics augmented their ideas by borrowing ready-made metaphysical systems from previous philosophers—the Epicureans took over the atomism of Democritus and the Stoics the *logos* and flux of Heraclitus—still the parts did not fit. For the fact was that they were interested only in themselves and not in the constitution of the world.

There is a way, however, in which the three philosophies can be defended. Instead of holding only one philosophy to the exclusion of all the others, suppose that each individual was equipped with many philosophies, and could rely on the one that was most appropriate when he found himself in a particular situation. Philosophy then, we could claim, speaking broadly and in the round, is mood music, and we become accustomed to using the philosophy that fits the mood, whatever it is. There are times of adversity, for example, when a man is called upon to show Stoic strength, other times when Epicurean serenity would be more fitting, and still other times of wild speculation and mystical belief when a Skeptical attitude would be most fitting.

The three philosophies we have just been discussing are by no means the only ones, and their acceptance does not lead to the only attitudes which it is possible to take. Philosophies are varied and many, as we shall see as we make our way slowly through the history of western philosophy. But in addition to mood philosophy every individual has a sort of major philosophy which fits him and which he wears most of the time when he is relaxed and off duty. For each of us philosophy is part of the life-style.

I am not suggesting that we try on philosophies for size, and wear only the one we feel most comfortable in. We grow up inside a philosophy. Our most fundamental beliefs are formed early and without our knowing about them, because we all are subjected to the same cultural environment and the same social influences. However, philosophies do come in different shapes and sizes, and to some extent at least we can put them on and off deliberately. We can, so to speak, see a little how things look from inside them.

This is not so easy to do with those enormously complex philosophies which call on a great deal of concentration to master, philosophies like those of Plato and Aristotle, of Kant and Hegel, for example. But there are others, on the other hand, which are quite simple. Let me give you an extreme example of the latter.

Suppose I were to announce, "All is one." That, I would argue, is a philosophy. It is consistent because it has no conflicting parts, and it is complete because nothing is left out. It thus meets two of the requirements of any system. But it does not meet a third requirement: it does not explain very much. What it does explain it explains clearly enough, but the explanation is so enormously simple that too many details slip through, and so while we may or may not reject it as a statement, we certainly cannot consider it sufficient as a philosophy.

At the other extreme, the extreme of utter complexity, we might have to make an exhaustive inventory of the contents of the whole world, listing everything and trying to find every connection. In that case we would never come to the end of our catalogue and surely would never be able to put the parts together. Somewhere between these two extremes lie all of the philosophies we are considering in this book.

If I wanted to show you how subtle and how difficult all philosophy is at the end, I might now ask, "Who says that all of the parts of the world *can* fit together, that there is in fact a system of the whole, could one only discover it?" At this point I leave you with your bewilderment, as with a job well done, because puzzlement is the beginning of curiosity, and curiosity leads to inquiry.

Chapter VI

The Era of
Religious Philosophy

In 474 B.C. the Romans founded a Republic. Rome already was a power when the Romans took over from the Greek generals of the Hellenistic period. By 146 B.C. they had gained the mastery of the entire Mediterranean, including of course the Greek city-states. The enemies of the Romans—the Macedonians who had been ruling Greece, the Carthaginians in North Africa and the Etruscans north of Rome in Italy—all were destroyed.

The Romans were not interested in abstract speculation, they were men of action, masters of practical affairs. They had a talent for organization and theirs was a great cultural achievement. They built an empire that lasted for many centuries. Administration on such a vast scale over such a vast domain required ease of communication. Accordingly they invented concrete and constructed roads so well that some of them are still usable.

Their ability to rule was so magnificent that one king bequeathed his country to Rome, on the theory that henceforth it would be better run. The Roman Empire covered the then known world, and extended from what is now Turkey on the east to Spain on the west. It became so large that it had to be split into two administrative wings, an eastern wing based in Constantinople and a western one based in Rome.

The Romans had little that was distinctively their own in the area of the arts. All of their literature, their painting, sculpture, theatre and architecture, was heavily influenced by what the Greeks had done before them. But they had won so much territory that they spread Greek culture more widely than the Greeks themselves had ever done.

Like the Alexandrian generals, the Romans took Greek culture with them wherever they went. That is one of the reasons we still have it. They preserved and translated Greek books and taught from them in schools. They also imitated them in their own writings. It has been pointed out that the first half of Vergil's *Aeneid* relies heavily on the *Iliad* of Homer and the second half relies on the *Odyssey*. The plays of the Romans, of Seneca, for instance, are almost all rewrites of Greek plays.

A comparison has been made between the small but creative Greek culture and the large Roman and Byzantine civilizations which spread it everywhere. You must not forget that Greek culture had two wings. It had the west Roman Empire and it also had that Empire's Byzantine Greek wing. In modern times there is a parallel with the culture of western Europe, which has been very creative, and the large American and Russian civilizations which have taken over European culture and extended its benefits to millions.

Let me give you an example of what I mean. I will take it from more recent times to show the spread of European culture to the United States. More than a hundred years ago Faraday in England made the first dynamo. It was a small affair indeed and he put it together in his wife's kitchen. Nowadays General Electric in Schenectady, New York, turns out huge ones on a belt line, each so large that it towers over a man.

There is a place for both small cultures and large civilizations in the broad scheme of things; a place for the small culture that is originative and inventive and for the large civilization which discovers nothing but which spreads the benefits discovered by the culture to the millions of people who need them. Progress is neither a steady nor a straight line affair. There are even backward periods when the gains are forgotten and the benefits lost.

The history of the Roman Empire may be called a long consolidation period in the account of western civilization. The Romans borrowed almost everything and preserved much, but added little. There was of course Roman law. There simply was no Roman philosophy, and that is why histories of philosophy are compelled to skip from Greece to the Middle Ages in Europe. That is not to say of course that philosophy was not highly regarded. Greek philosophy was studied and preserved and it was part of the equipment of every educated Roman that he had been trained in Greek philosophy. Yet from the point of view of the history of philosophy, it was a long pause.

That pause was broken by an interesting new development. Before I can tell you about it I must remind you of something. In ancient Greece philosophical speculation was free. Despite the martyrdom of Socrates, which took place in the name of reason rather than religion, the philosophers were allowed to think whatever they wished. No one attempted to set bounds to their thoughts.

When a change came, it was the result of a new wave of religion, one that ended in the establishment of a church which was destined to curb speculation.

In the first century A.D. there were important developments in religious philosophy which were to influence men for thousands of years. The force which precipitated these developments came from another religious influence. Greek culture and the Jewish religion met headlong in North Africa.

Cultural developments are often the result of the coming together of civilizations which had developed independently and which had somehow to be reconciled. The Jews with their religion and their civilization had been established in what we now call the Middle East long before the great age of Greece.

Alexandria, the port of Egypt, was a center of culture. It was founded by Alexander the Great, and later gathered together the greatest scholars ever assembled in one place. The Alexandrian library, later burned by Christian mobs, had the largest collection of books of any library in ancient times. Philosophers came from all over and discussed their favorite fields of inquiry. Among those who were brought together in this fashion were Greek philosophers from Athens and Jewish scholars who came originally from Palestine.

Philo, the Jewish scholar, was born in Alexandria twenty years before Jesus. Although he was a contemporary of John the Baptist and of St. Paul, it is doubtful that he knew anything about them. What he did know about, and that in great detail, was the Bible and the Jewish religion. He was a pious Jew, but he was also a scholar, the first Jewish scholar, perhaps, to learn about Greek philosophy.

The two most powerful sources of western civilization, it is generally agreed, were Jewish morality and Greek reason. The essence of the practice of the Jewish religion was its morality. What the Greek philosophers agreed about was the use of reason. These two great instruments of human culture, morality and reason, passed into the hands of the Europeans and contributed in no small way to their force and effectiveness.

When two systems meet, if you want to combine them, something has to give way. Now Philo was not prepared to give up anything of the Jewish religion, which he considered an inspiration from God. The Jewish religious truths were absolute truths. How then was he to reconcile them with Greek philosophy?

Philo hit upon two new methods, which have been followed by many thinkers ever since. If you will allow me to speak of Plato's philosophy as the best representative of Hellenism, then Philo was able to combine Hellenism with Judaism by modifying Hellenism whenever they conflicted. They did not always conflict of course, for if they had then the making of a whole out of the two would have been impossible. But there were points on which agreement could be seen.

Plato had held that the highest form of human life is the intellectual life, the contemplation of the Ideas. Philo asserted much the same thing, though he tended to regard it as thinking God's thoughts after Him. The accent is certainly different, though there is here no essential conflict. When Philo and Plato did differ, however, then for Philo the word of God was to be preferred to the word of a mere philosopher even if the name of that philosopher was Plato.

And so Philo's first method for reconciling Hellenism with Judaism was to make the first subservient to the second. For Philo philosophy was not quite as free as the Greeks had contended. It is the purpose of philosophy, he thought, to serve the faith. This it could do by defending religious doctrine and by arguing against its enemies.

The second method that Philo hit upon has been called the *allegorical method*. Let me give an example. If man were an independent unit, Philo argued, then man could be alone. But only God can be alone, and therefore God is the principle of unity. Again, speaking of the pleasures of the Garden of Eden, Philo said that they were "intended symbolically rather than literally," a method of "making ideas visible," for the forms of things existed in the Divine Mind before the things themselves did.

Philo was continually engaged in making philosophical deductions from Scripture, but there can be little doubt that he thought religion superior. At the same time, philosophy had its rightful place in his scheme of things. Every story in the Old Testament was interpreted to mean something abstract. The creation of Eve in the Garden of Eden is not to be taken literally, Philo insisted, as indeed nothing in Scripture is. It is a "myth," showing that sense perception has its point of origin when the human mind is asleep. The bringing of Woman to Man meant for Philo the introduction of Sense Perception to Mind, which recognizes it as its own.

Philo's method of allegory and his use of reason to reinforce revelation, or in other words of philosophy to reinforce Scripture, was to have a long history. One of Philo's students was a man named Ammonius Saccas, who had a pupil named Plotinus. It was from Plotinus that St. Augustine, in the fourth century A.D., learned how to construct a theology for Christianity. From there the influence is easy to trace because it is unmistakable.

The philosophy which Philo derived from Plato by making appropriate changes was henceforth called "Neoplatonism." Neoplatonism, as set forth by Philo, differed from Platonism in at least three important respects.

The first of these was that the Ideas, which Plato thought had their own domain, were in fact according to Philo thoughts in the Mind of God.

The second of the ways in which Neoplatonism differed from Platonism was in the nature of matter, which Philo but not Plato considered evil.

The third way in which they differed was over the source of creation, which in Philo (but not in Plato) occurred from a spilling over of God's abundant goodness.

These differences are important enough to warrant talking about them a little more.

Plato explained the existence of abstract Ideas, or as we have since come to call them, *universals,* by asserting that they had their own domain in which they are eternal. Round *things* may be destroyed: balloons can burst, balls can bounce, suns, as we now know, sometimes explode. But circularity is sure to last forever as a universal which is always possible of exemplification in matter.

Philo did not deny any of this. He merely asserted that instead of being independent affairs the Ideas were thoughts in the Divine Mind. For Plato the gods had become divine through the contemplation of the Ideas, and so the Ideas came first. Philo reversed this and put God first, with the Ideas reduced to the condition of being merely His thoughts.

Philo supposed that matter is evil in itself, and human beings are inclined toward evil by their sensuous or material natures. But for Plato matter is not evil, it is partly real and partly merely an appearance. Evil as a matter of fact was not a word the Greeks possessed, or if they did they did not think of it in connection with God. Evil for the Greeks was the same as error, and error lay in missing the mark.

Creation, according to Plato, was the work of God, but He accomplished it by using a model which already existed before Him, a model which consisted in the Ideas. For Plato material things, as we have already noted, owed their reality to their resemblance to the Ideas, of which therefore they were copies. But that implied the existence of something beside God for which He was not entirely responsible, namely, the domain of abstract Ideas. And so Philo felt obliged to modify this view by asserting that in the beginning there was nothing but God, who had made the world out of Himself, from the abundance of his own goodness as it spilled over.

In all three doctrines it is plain that Philo turned a natural philosophy into a religious philosophy, one in which God played a much bigger role. If God is the only principle of unity, then God is the whole of which all parts are parts. But, it would be fair to ask Philo, "How can the whole be made into a principle of explanation, which must distinguish between the parts, when on this theory they are equally parts of the same whole in the same way?"

The answer that Philo would have to make, I suppose, is that he *did* distinguish between the parts. God's abundant goodness spilled over in layers, as it were. The highest layer next to God Himself contained the Ideas, then came the *Logos* (the totality of the Ideas), The Divine Spirit (later to be called The Holy Ghost), the Angels, Man, and, finally, matter.

At every layer there was a desire and an effort to get back to God and to be united once again with Him. Man strove ever upward toward God in virtue of his spirit, but since he was also half matter he was pulled downward toward evil.

The change Philo brought about in the thought of subsequent generations was a radical one. The understanding of Plato as a secular philosopher has been obscured ever since. Philo also turned a free enterprise into a controlled one. This was the beginning of theology, the philosophy of religion, a mythologized philosophy in which it is assigned an inferior second place to religion. It was to be a very long time before philosophy succeeded in shaking itself free from religion, though, as we shall see, many centuries later the new dominant institution became that of physical science and the philosophical enslavement became a voluntary affair.

The cheapest thing in the world, as it turns out, is the "absolute truth." Everybody has one. So many people are sure they are in possession of the right one that they think nothing of imposing it on others. That would do very well were it not for the fact that conceptions of the absolute truth differ so widely. One man's truth is the ground for another man's skepticism. I once defined a "fanatic" as a man who believes in the truth of some *other* religion. As we noted earlier in connection with the Greek religions, the very word "myth" usually means the beliefs of some religion other than our own, which its adherents hold to be the absolute truth. If we could remember that the other fellow's religious beliefs are only myths to one who does not hold them, it might save us from more religious wars, which have proved time and again to be as vicious as any.

All three of the great western world religions employed the same method once Philo showed the way. Philo, as we have already noted, through his pupil, Ammonius Saccas, taught Plotinus, and Plotinus thought that he could defend Greek religion, the religion of Zeus and the other gods, by means of Neoplatonism, the new version of Plato's philosophy, in a way that the Greeks themselves had never done. Similarly, St. Augustine used Neoplatonism to defend Christianity, and a few centuries later Al Fārābi used Neoplatonism to defend the new religion of Islam.

Augustine, as a matter of fact, accomplished more than that. He had some original ideas and enough sweep to be called one of the great philosophers. He tried to show that belief and knowledge are interdependent; without the one, he said, you could not have the other. He gave the first argument for the existence of God when he identified Aristotle's "first cause" with God, which Aristotle himself of course had not done.

But most important of all for our purposes, he began the topic which later came to be called the philosophy of history, a theory that history has a form which can be detected in the shape of events. In his book *The City of God* he made a philosophical interpretation of Adam and Eve in the Garden of Eden, and of the rest of the story. He went on to explain that there is a City of God and a City of the Devil, the former being composed of man's virtues, the other of his vices. A sharp reader will see in The City of God echoes of Plato's Ideas and in the City of the Devil echoes of the material world in space and time.

What Augustine showed was that history can be described in narrative form, and that such narratives can be interpreted philosophically. He extended Philo's ideas in a way which demonstrated that the allegorical method could be extended to the whole of history. Later his method was revised so that the Ideas which are imbedded in history could be abstracted and exhibited as a philosophy of history.

Social revolutions do not occur over night. Rome had fallen to the German invaders led by Alaric, King of the Visigoths, in 410 A.D., and by 476 the most powerful of the German generals in Italy had banished the last emperor of the west and were themselves for all practical purposes fully in control of western Europe. The German conquerors mingled freely with the conquered and intermarried with them. Only the Christian Church under the domination of the Papacy retained any semblance of organization, but no general government appeared until Charlemagne, the Frankish king, put together an Empire briefly, in 771.

After that the breakdown resulted in the petty principalities of the feudal order, which is better described as an age of disorder. Popes struggled with kings for control, and it was not until the rise of the modern nation states that the secular powers were able to win out completely. In the east there was a different situation, for there the remnants of the Orthodox Christian Empire held out in Constantinople for a thousand years, until 1453, in fact.

It is no wonder that orderly thought was not pursued when social conditions were as bad as they were. The Frankish king, Charlemagne, had endeavored to establish some sort of order in Europe, and he succeeded but only partially and for a brief while. The social order was not an order properly speaking but a series of local arrangements which resembled one another. There were many principalities, and these were divided into great estates centered on castles and surrounded by lands whose farmers, called "serfs" were attached to the land and its owner and could not be removed from it, a form of slavery in which certain rights were reserved to the slaves. The lord of the castle had the duty to protect his serfs but he in turn could call on them for military service.

All that these district-states had in common was the Christian religion, but that religion dominated the social and political life of Europe for the next thousand years. Under this dispensation philosophy was subordinated to faith, but reason does not work well in harness.

The transition from Roman civilization to the Christian civilization of medieval Europe required hundreds of years to complete. On balance, it marked a cultural loss rather than a gain; a gain in ideals perhaps, but a loss in practice. As we have noted already, the feudal system which prevailed for many centuries was distinguished by small landholders who had serfs to work the land, and who engaged in an endless series of neighborhood wars.

What the masses succeeded in doing, if indeed they had any hand in the change at all, was to exchange the Roman aristocracy for the aristocracy of the Roman Catholic Church and the lords of the medieval principalities, and finally for the rulers of many small kingdoms. In the struggle for power that followed between the Popes and the Kings, the people were not consulted and in any case had little to gain.

Revolutions are not always advances. Often the poor and

ignorant remain poor and ignorant, and find that they have succeeded only in exchanging one set of masters for another. Tolstoy once remarked that the rich would do anything for the poor except get off their backs. If we will substitute the word "powerful" for "rich," then it is just as true of the heads of the communist government of the Soviet Union as it is of the heads of industry under capitalism. If we look back from the period in which we live, we can see a gain; but this is usually a result of the fact that we ourselves happen to be among the benefactors.

So long as social organizations are necessary, there will always have to be a ruling class, though its personnel and its forms of power change; wealth, caste or political skill, it is all the same in the end. The only difference with which we should remain concerned is whether that ruling class sees its advantages in terms of obligation or only of privilege.

Not for nothing, then, has the period from the spread of Christianity to the rise of science, roughly from the fourth century A.D. to the fourteenth, been called "the age of faith." Do you remember where I tried to show the relative importance to the Greeks of nature, man and God? Well, for the age of faith that has to be changed. God was now much larger in the picture and man was a small part of God. Nature was even smaller and stood not only below but on the outside.

The greatest strength of a religion is what it can explain, not how much it can comfort. Christians will tell you that faith in Christianity is comforting, and so no doubt it is. But so is the Jewish faith, so is the Moslem faith, and many others. A little examination will show that all faiths are equally comforting, which ought to tell you something about faith. With respect to the comfort afforded by faith, there is no reason to choose one over another! Therefore explanation is more important.

A faith is a kind of emotional conviction of the truth of a belief. A religion is such a set of beliefs, and no matter how silly these may appear to a non-believer, they are comforting to the believer. And so it is impossible to argue from the strength of a faith to the truth of a belief. Belief in what is false will serve to comfort equally with what is true so long as it is a belief and the object of a faith.

That faith was the basis for the founding of the Roman Catholic Church. I hope my readers can distinguish between a religion and a church. For religion, individual belief is quite sufficient, but for a church an institution is required.

It might be helpful at this point if I set forth the elements of a church. Every church has a text containing a *creed* or revelation. This leads to a general *morality*, whose observance is dramatized by a *ritual*, and overseen, and even in some cases reinforced, by a *clergy*. A church, in other words, is the social and institutional version of a religion.

After Augustine, whose dates were 354 to 430, there fell a long dry period in western civilization. For a thousand years of Christianity, nothing much happened in the way of thought. There were other developments of course, chiefly religious; the building of the Gothic cathedrals, for instance. But there was no new philosophy. Not for nothing is this period, which is usually called the Middle Ages, often known also as the Dark Ages. For a general illiteracy prevailed. No one knew how to read and write except the monks in their monasteries. They get a much-deserved credit for keeping learning alive, but at the same time they did nothing to spread it. There was no attempt at universal education. Instead, as one might have expected, there was dirt and there were diseases, often of epidemic proportions.

Strictly speaking, an account of European philosophy ought to be accompanied by a detailed account of European history. This cannot be given here for want of space, but the outlines are clear enough. In addition to the spread of the monastic orders, there was the rise of the Papacy, the endless wars, and the feudal system of enslavement. Piety was widespread, but so also were poverty, filth and disease. Many of the Popes engaged in worldly struggles with the temporal powers, and constituted themselves political forces inconsistent with the otherworldliness of the Church. The Holy Roman Empire, which had been destined to replace the older Roman Empire, did not hold together for very long. Outside the Church there was no rule of order, only an order based on brute strength. This was not enough to protect Christendom from its enemies.

Subsequent centuries saw the rise of Islam after the amazing success of Mohammed in the seventh century, and the conquest by the Moslems under his successors of most of the countries of the eastern Mediterranean. By the year 1353 the Ottoman Turks had gained a foothold in Europe. Spain and half of Italy were ruled by Moslems. Christian slaves were sold in the markets of Venice. The Turks were not defeated until the siege of Vienna in 1683, after which they were never again important in world politics.

The later Middle Ages seemed to do no more than intensify the ills of the earlier period. Countries became larger and wars bigger, the bubonic plague and epidemics of smallpox and cholera decimated the population and contributed to the general disorder, unrest and despair.

Philosophy rarely ever appears on the surface, that is, in the thoughts of philosophers and their books, although the exceptions to this statement make up its known history. It tends to lurk rather in social institutions and their struggle for supremacy, in familiar customs and moral practices. In these and other ways, such as in questions of taste and in avowed goals, it influences people without their recognizing its nature. Social shifts in philosophy are rarely deliberate.

The Christian monks preserved and studied the best of Greek philosophy. But they were careful to concentrate on its literary and humanistic sides. Its scientific side they left strictly alone. Aristotle had written scientific treatises on psychology, on physics and astronomy, and on other topics. And there were of course the records left by the mathematicians and the experimental scientists such as Archimedes, Appolonius of Perga and many others. But the early monks were not interested. Why be concerned with the things of this world when it was only the next world that counted?

We would never have known of the scientific works of the

Greeks had it not been for Moslem civilization. The Ottoman Empire, based in Constantinople (now called Istanbul), became not only a military bastion but also a tremendous center of learning. The Moslem scholars preserved, translated and edited many of the Greek scientific works.

It is hard to understand how Moslem civilization rose to such heights. For the practices of the Ottoman Turks were in many ways peculiar to themselves. For instance, they stole Christian children and raised them to be the rulers of Islam while at the same time these rulers remained slaves. Hardest of all to believe, perhaps, is the tolerance which the Moslems exercised with respect to religious beliefs, at least part of the time and in some places. In the twelfth century in Cardova, Spain, there lived both the Arab philosopher, Averroës, and the Jewish philosopher, Maimonides. Even harder to believe, they were personal friends.

They had a new plan for religious philosophy. Perhaps the work of Aristotle, which was much more down-to-earth than that of Plato, could be used to modify the Neoplatonic versions of their religion. Perhaps, in other words, reason and, still better, the sense experience in which Aristotle had believed so firmly, could be used to make Neoplatonic religions more practical.

Neoplatonism could serve in almost its pure state to support religious revelations, and we have seen that early on it was so used. It was used by the Greeks, the Christians and the Jews, with the Jews, led by Philo, showing the way to the others. But now, more than a thousand years later, an even more powerful system was put together, again by all three religions, using the philosophy of Aristotle with its emphasis on sense experience, to modify the Neoplatonic version of revelation. This time it was done by Averroës for the Arabs, by Maimonides for the Jews and, a hundred years later, and openly using the work of these two scholars for a model, by St. Thomas Aquinas for the Christians.

It was not quite the smooth sailing for the philosophy of Aquinas that one is sometimes led to believe. His work at first was officially condemned, and he was not canonized until many centuries later. Shortly after his death in 1274 his work was condemned both at Paris and Oxford. In the next few hundred years the reputation of his work shifted from one extreme to the other. In 1879 Pope Leo XIII directed that his philosophy should be made the basis of all Catholic theology. His philosophy now is the "approved" philosophy of the Roman Catholic Church, not the official philosophy, for there is none.

Aquinas made a distinction which was damaging to Christian theology, though that was not his intention. He separated "natural theology" from "revealed theology" and said that while the revealed variety could not be questioned, the former could. Now since they revolved often about the same issues, the distinction was an odd one. Take the issue of God's existence, for instance. As "revealed," this was something a good Roman Catholic was not allowed to question but must take on faith. As "natural," however, he could doubt it, argue about it, or do whatever he pleased. Both questions could occur in the same connection, and it is difficult to see how two conflicting answers could be accepted.

The object of the distinction was to place forever beyond question the dogma of the Church. But that is not what the distinction actually accomplished. What it did was to expose the dogma to examination. And under the new freedoms of reason and sense experience, and the new tests of logic and experiment, some of the dogma did not stand up so well.

There were other new developments at the time. The Crusades, which were Christian expeditions sent from Europe to the Middle East in the twelfth and thirteenth centuries to free Palestine, the "holy land," from the infidel, were miserable failures. But, like so many social events, they had effects which had not been foreseen. Some of the defeated Crusaders came back with loot, and among the loot were to be found Arabic translations of early Greek scientific works.

For a long time men had not taken the material world too seriously, and they had what appeared to them to be good reasons. For one thing, matter itself (you will remember) was considered evil and so the material world was an evil place. For another thing, since it was the next world and not this one that counted, there was no point in dealing with this world except as a preparation.

Not this life but the expected life after death was the one to be taken seriously, and whether you went to heaven and a life of eternal bliss or to hell and a life of eternal damnation depended upon how many of the pleasures of this world you could manage to avoid. The Christian Middle Ages were based on a denial of earthly life and a hope of immortality.

Chapter VII

The Return to
the Material World

There is an excellent book by a man with a beautiful Irish name, DeLacy O'Leary, and it is entitled *How Greek Science Passed to the Arabs*. It tells the unique story about the way in which the Moslem civilization received and preserved the Greek scientific works and, when the time came, handed them on to Christian Europe. If the knowledge of Greek science had not been transmitted to the Arabs, in all likelihood we would not have it today.

You may recall that the Roman Empire had been so large that it had had to be split into two administrative wings, one based in Rome of course and the other based in Constantinople (now named Istanbul). When Christianity took over from the Roman Empire, we have noted, it followed the same split: the Roman Catholic Church in the west and the Greek Orthodox Christian Church in the east. In time the two Churches had a quarrel so violent that each solemnly and formally pronounced a curse on the other. Since the Renaissance, the Roman Catholics and the Protestants have done their best to forget the existence of the third great wing of Christianity, even though it is as old and as official as the Roman Catholic.

The Greek Orthodox branch of Christianity ran into very bad luck. Constantinople, and indeed the whole of the Middle East, including Egypt and extending as far to the west as Persia and beyond, was overrun by the Arabs with their new Moslem religion and their new institutions and scientific learning. We shall see later that the bad luck was repeated in modern times, for the Russians had been long established Greek Orthodox Christians when the Communist Revolution occurred there in 1917.

The Greek scientific works told the Arabs the story of how sense experience could be extended by means of instruments and reasoning by means of mathematics. There was a formal way of forcing nature to answer a question by conducting a planned experiment in which observation would play a leading role. This meant attending once again to what things are like in this world for their own sake rather than for what they could tell us about the next.

The way had already been prepared by religious philosophers who never dreamed what the effects of their speculations would be. Since Aquinas had authorized natural theology, speculations about nature, at least, could once again be free. Some of the scholarly monks, men like Roscellinus in the eleventh century, but chiefly in the period we are talking about now, the fourteenth century, such thinkers as William of Occam, agreed that universals do not exist except as thoughts in the human mind. What does exist they said are material things, which are always particulars. "Occam's Razor" came to be the name for a famous principle that there should be no more universals than were called for in order to name things, no more, Occam said, than were necessary.

The new learning had a direct bearing on the old faith. If universals were not the most real things, then neither was Church dogma. The Church of course finally awoke to the danger and fought back, but by then it was almost too late. The new developments were moving too fast and yielding results which were too exciting. When men looked naively at the material world, what they saw, as though for the first time, was dazzling. Led by monks like Robert Grosseteste and Roger Bacon, the full scientific method was rediscovered and with it the importance of mathematics as the language of science.

If philosophy was to remain in the picture, its allegiance would have to be changed. It would no longer have to be subservient to the Church but now would have to square with scientific findings. Experience henceforth would be verified by planned experiments with their mathematically-expressed results.

So much for the physical world. But there was also the rediscovery of man himself. He was no longer to be considered merely the source of an immortal soul which was important only because it could be separated from his body at death. He was to the contrary an interesting thing in his own right, here and now, complete with his mind and body. This part of the new movement, called "humanism," was destined to transform every corner of social life.

The language of all philosophy and indeed of all serious concerns had been Latin, which the priests alone knew. Very few others could write at all, but now writing began in the "vulgar" languages of the common people, in French, English, German and indeed in all the European languages. Men for the first time were able to compose literary works in the language they used for ordinary purposes.

The period as a whole, fully underway by the fifteenth century, was known as the Renaissance, a word taken from the French and meaning "rebirth"—the rebirth, as it were, of Greek culture. The Greek interest in nature, and in man as part of nature, had been expressed not only in scientific works but also in the arts, in sculpture and architecture, and above all in drama. The beauty of the human form, and the remorseless logic of events illustrated in the Greek drama, were brought home to men with something of a shock, and no less so because it was a shock of delight.

All of a sudden men were discovering that this world was a

place of intense interest and pleasure in every corner, and a lot larger than anyone had supposed. Investigations were conducted into the composition of the human body by painters and sculptors in Italy, primarily in Florence, and explorations were undertaken of the unknown world across the seas.

In the sky astronomy was making revolutionary new advances. For thousands of years it had been supposed that the earth was the center of the universe, with the stars either fixed or revolving around it. This was the geocentric system of Ptolemy, and it served well those who wished to elevate man to a position more important than anything else in the world and second only to God.

Now Copernicus and later Galileo, with his new instrument, the telescope, and Kepler were able to demonstrate that the earth was not the center of the solar system but instead revolved around the sun, thus suggesting a new heliocentric system.

A serious blow was dealt by these new scientific findings to the authority of the Roman Catholic Church. The world picture which it had been defending was shattered for once and all. If the earth revolved around the sun, Heaven could no longer be up and Hell down, because "up" and "down" continually exchanged places. Man was clearly no longer at the center of the universe, and therefore *not* nearest to God.

More damage still was done by the decline of the morality of the clergy. There was widespread sexual activity on the part of priests and nuns, and the corruption extended even to the Pope himself. Alexander VI, the Pope who was a member of the rich and powerful but notorious Borgia family, filled the Vatican with troops of boys and girls for his own sexual entertainment. He even defended the practice when he said, "Since God has given us the Papacy, let us enjoy it." Under the circumstances of such widespread immorality there was bound to be a growing resentment and indeed a revolt.

In the fifteenth century and the first half of the sixteenth in Western Europe, reformers like Luther, Zwingli and Calvin broke away from the Church and led the movement into separatist churches which still held themselves to be Christian—more Christian, in fact, than the Catholics, because for their doctrine they returned to the origins of Christianity.

The new Protestant religions were bitterly fought by the Catholics. In a series of wars in the sixteenth century both sides brutally butchered each other and did not spare either women or children, thus offering strong evidence that the Jesus of *Matthew* 22 had few followers. In the Thirty Years' War both Catholics and Protestants wiped out thousands of villages, killing all their inhabitants and burning them to the ground. Germany was more than decimated, in some places the population was reduced to less than half, and the atrocities committed by the soldiers of all nations was a commonplace. When Nietzsche later said that the last Christian died on the cross, it was very nearly true. Brotherly love has rarely existed in the world.

Gradually peace and order was restored by a kind of truce which saw the two sides tolerating if not loving each other. In 1534 the Church of England, which preserved the Catholic forms, declared itself independent of Rome. The Edict of Nantes was a law promulgated in April 1598 by the French King, Henry IV, which secured a large measure of religious liberty to his Protestant subjects, the Huguenots.

The Protestant movement had brought about the autonomy of the individual. Now for the first time man could communicate with God without benefit of clergy. A Protestant Church was a collection of worshippers each of whom had his own individual access to God. He was no longer bound to any dogma and could interpret Christian doctrine as he chose. He could read the Bible for himself. It was no help to the Roman Catholic Church that it fought back by means of reforms, and particularly by the establishment of the Inquisition, a court of clergy which sat in judgment on defectors from the true faith and handed the worst of these over to the civil authorities to be burned at the stake.

For individualism had been discovered and the precious freedoms it brought would now be cherished and increased. When in 1600 Giordano Bruno was executed by burning, it was for holding beliefs which are commonplace now. But others soon took his place. And if he entertained the heresy that God and the universe were opposite sides of the same coin, since God was simply the unity of the universe, it was only what later thinkers were to assert in greater safety. The martyrdom of Bruno to the truth of science was exacted by the Church as the price of opposition, but the new wave of enthusiasm for sense experience was not to be stopped.

We shall read in the next chapter about the writings of Spinoza, who extended his piety to include the material world. Following Bruno he saw it as only another aspect of God, thus easing the transition from the classic religious view to a new scientific one. The distinguished American religious scholar, Harry A. Wolfson, has pointed out the part that the Jews played in forming the Middle Ages. Philo, he said, invented the scholastic method and Spinoza ended it. There is a bit of truth in that statement.

When belief is first freed from the chains of faith, it runs wild as though drunk with its new liberty. All sorts of beliefs, all kinds of mysticism, are accepted in one quarter or another. But gradually sanity reasserts itself, and a new set of principles is adopted. The new ones this time were to be based on reason and fact. Francis Bacon not only tried to establish the scientific method as a firm way of investigating nature, he also attacked the old habits and prejudices, the ancient traditions and authorities, especially the authority of Aristotle, whose followers had for many centuries regarded his answers as final in a way Aristotle himself never had.

It was not until the late sixteenth and early seventeenth centuries that the first modern materialist, Thomas Hobbes, was able to state and develop his position. The three kinds of reality, he said, were *space*, *body* and *motion*, not unlike the old *matter*, *motion* and the *void* of Leucippus and Democritus. God must exist, he admitted, but his nature is undiscoverable. The rest of religion can be satisfied by seeking the answers to man's curiosity about natural phenomena.

Perhaps his greatest contribution, however, lay in the field of politics, which was now beginning to be studied again, as it seldom had been since Plato and Aristotle. Hobbes was the author of what has come since to be called the "social contract." If all natural rights were exercised, society would be impossible, he declared, for as he pointed out, all men seek unlimited individual power. If left alone this could only result in what he described as "a war of all against all."

Since such a war would have produced an impossible social situation, men had deliberately sought a method of achieving peaceful coexistence, which, he thought, was "the first law of [human] nature." Peace was achieved through Hobbes' second law by a "mutual transferring of right" in "that which men call contract," to "be contented with so much liberty against other men as he would allow himself." In short, the very existence of society suggests that men had voluntarily entered into a contract to transfer the use of power to the state, in which they could then live peacefully together.

No such contract is known to have been made in historical time. It is a figure of speech to describe the conditions which prevail as premises in every society in order for there to be a society in the first place. Broadly speaking, however, it would perhaps be fair to claim that every constitution or charter which had been deliberately established, such as for instance the Constitution of the United States adopted in Philadelphia in 1791 amounts to such a social contract.

Hobbes was no democrat, however. He believed in an absolute monarchy, and declared that only a king with unlimited powers would be able to identify himself with the common good. The king could be opposed, should he fail to serve the common good, and thus there could be some sort of check upon his abuse of power.

The return to the material world was now officially begun and

Hobbes' philosophy was the first comprehensive expression of it. That world, as man was to discover, is a wide one, and its investigation is still in progress. We have extended the inquiry not only to the complexity of man himself in one direction but also to the vastness of the solar system in another. You can see how very wide it is.

Chapter VIII

Knowledge from Reasoning Alone

The scientific movement had a strong impact on every corner of European civilization, which it was destined in a short few hundred years to transform completely. But it began slowly, and though in the early seventeenth century it was not yet widespread, it was felt by sensitive and intuitive men almost immediately. One of them was Descartes. It is surprising to remember now that his dates were almost the same as Galileo's. But before turning to his work and the work of others who felt the same influences, let me introduce the large problem of being in somewhat broader terms.

To the basic philosophical question, "What is it all about?" Plato, you will recall, said that there are three and only three ways of finding out. Plato endeavored to employ all three in his philosophy. He explained what they are in a myth about a charioteer who drives two horses. The charioteer stands for reason, one of the horses stands for the disciplined emotions and the other for the unruly appetite. We would say the capacity for thought, the ability to feel, and the impulse to action. These can be employed in any preferred order.

We shall next see that a seventeenth century group of philosophers on the European mainland preferred to work with thought primarily. A somewhat later group, beginning in the seventeenth century but extending well into the eighteenth, were Englishmen who preferred sense experience, and in particular the sense of sight. Much later still, in the nineteenth century, a group of American philosophers calling themselves "pragmatists," after the word for *practice*, preferred action. But that is getting somewhat ahead of our story.

It occurred to each of these groups of philosophers to see how far it was possible to go in the total explanation of man, God and the world, employing thought, emotion and action only one at a time. It would be foolish not to argue that they had other experiences to call on, but they planned to bring them in afterwards. Anything that the first group had learned from sense experience or practice would have to be used only after a base had been established by means of reason. In so doing they were in a way being faithful to the philosophical tradition, for every philosopher begins by undertaking an explanation which is utterly simple. What position would you arrive at, they wondered, just by thinking about the problem and by taking nothing at all for granted?

René Descartes tried to get along with reasoning alone, without appealing to the evidence of the senses or the evidence of practice. He had a plan which was suggested to him by something Augustine had written. In order to be answerable only to reason, it would first be necessary to clear the mind of all belief, to start over, as it were, with a blank page and to write on it only what could not be denied. I will do just that, Descartes resolved. I will begin with a state of absolute doubt to which there are no exceptions. But doubt, he went on, is predicated on thought: to doubt is after all to think. I doubt, therefore I think. Well now at least I have admitted that much: I think. But I wanted to think about the most fundamental of all problems, the problem of what there is. But now, in order to think about this problem, the least thing I can recognize in existence is that I *think*. But if I think, then I must admit that it is *I* who thinks, and so I exist: *I think*, he said, *therefore I am*.

But who or what is responsible for my existence? Surely I did not make myself. It would not be unreasonable to conclude, therefore, that a being greater than myself made me, a being more perfect, complete, rational and moral—in a word, God. And so now we can say that God exists.

Now that Descartes had himself and God, in that order, it remained only to recover the world. Therefore he went on to argue as follows. My senses report the existence of an external world of material objects, a sensuous physical world. Can I trust my senses to this extent? His answer was: yes, but only for one reason: God gave me my senses, and if I could not trust them it would mean that God was a deceiver. But the idea of deception is inconsistent with the idea of a perfect God. Therefore God is not a deceiver and the external world that I perceive with the aid of my senses *does* exist.

Thus, beginning with universal doubt, Descartes was sure that he had ended by proving through reason alone not only the existence of himself but also of God and the world.

In the philosophy of Descartes there are several developments that are quite new, which you would not notice unless you examined his ideas very closely. One development is that according to Descartes reality—what there is—is derived from the way in which we learn about it. And we learn about it by thinking about it.

This brings us to the second development. When Descartes began by discussing man, it was not the whole man he wanted, only man's mind. Henceforth when he said "man" he meant "mind."

An entire revolution in philosophy was introduced in this innocent fashion, and it is by no means certain that Descartes was aware of the immense effect his distinctions were to have. For although Descartes was a pious Roman Catholic and had no idea of departing from Church doctrine, nevertheless that is precisely the effect of the ideas he introduced. God may have remained first and foremost in his affection, but just the same he dropped the idea of *God* as a principle of explanation. This left only the other two: *mind* and the *world*. The world to which Descartes referred was of course the material world, and so we can say more briefly for him, *mind* and *matter*. His exact words were, "thinking things and extended things."

Curiously, this led Descartes to deny what Plato had asserted so strongly: that the abstract Ideas we have called universals exist and that they are what men think about when they think abstractly. No, he insisted, universals exist only in minds as their thoughts and in matter as its forms. His version of experience was derived from *human thinking* and confined to it. This is what led him to insist that animals have no consciousness and are only machines.

Every new idea solves some problems, it also introduces new areas of ignorance. Thus while knowledge increases, so does the need for more knowledge, and we shall never see the end of it. For instance, a new science of psychology was made possible by raising the human mind in importance to the level of the material world. Unfortunately, part of that material world is the human body, which is where mind and matter first meet. What then is their relationship? Either they are equal and never meet, or mind is derived from matter, or matter is derived from mind. Each of these positions has been taken up and defended with all of its consequences by some philosopher or other. And the problem is even now still being debated.

So subtle is philosophy and so powerful its influence that for centuries it never occurred to anybody that reality did not have to be divided in exactly Descartes' way, and that in fact to so divide it might be false and misleading. When you consider that we are talking about the minds of human beings on a single small planet and that matter is coextensive with the cosmic universe, it hardly seems like an equal division. Furthermore, as we are coming to believe for experimental reasons, mind might be a property of one kind of very complicated matter composing the brain and the central nervous system. None of this of course was evident to Descartes, who had merely suggested the division.

But to return to Descartes, he was sure that the mind is not entirely free. It tends to operate in terms of fixed classifications, or *categories*. This was an idea later further developed by another famous philosopher, Immanuel Kant. The theory of truth that Descartes liked best—every philosopher has one—was the one suggested first by the Stoics. If you remember that Descartes by his own theory could not appeal to sense experience but had to derive everything we know from the human mind by the method of reasoning, his theory of truth was just what you might have imagined it had to be. The truth, he said, is what is clear and distinct. Falsehood, accordingly, is what is confused, unclear and indistinct.

As it happens, the human mind is not a primary source of knowledge. If you consider the problem a little bit, you will see that there has never been anything in the human mind, apart from the act of thought itself, that did not represent something in the external world, except for the capacity for thought and the production of error, and even the material for error came first from that world too. If you have the image of a chair in your mind, it is because you have examined real ones, say of wood or steel. But, on the other hand, if you have the image of a dog with wings, it is because you have seen both dogs and wings. The error of putting dogs and wings together is one you made for yourself, a pure product of your mind.

The influence of Descartes has been almost out of proportion to the amount of his writings. He did not write all that much. But he opened doors his successors poured through. He gave them a choice: they could investigate *mind* or they could investigate *matter*. The philosophers seized on mind as their special province; the new and brilliantly successful scientists chose matter.

This led to several developments that were nothing short of disastrous. One such development was that science split off from philosophy, which it had not done before, had not done, for example, in the period of the height of Greek culture, in the 5th and 4th centuries B.C. For each needs the other. Science needs philosophy to examine what it takes for granted; both in the assumptions of its experimental method and in the meaning of its discoveries. And philosophy needs science if it is to put all of knowledge together into any sort of inclusive system. A further development of the split between philosophy and science was that philosophy turned inward. By *mind* Descartes had meant the conscious mind, and so henceforth the philosophers concentrated on the nature of consciousness and its contents. But if it is true that there is little in the conscious mind that was not first in the external world, then the mind is not the best place in which to look for knowledge.

Also, and equally important, the *conscious* mind is not the whole story of the mind, as Freud was at pains to tell us much later and in another connection. There is also the *unconscious* mind and its storehouse of memories. The *unconscious* contains more than consciousness at any given time. It is what we used to refer to more simply as "memory." What you can recall—and you can recall a very great deal if you work at it—must exist somewhere in your brain until you recall it.

The unconscious mind has important links to the rest of the body, links which are so intimate that perhaps the division is not justified. The link to the brain is particularly intimate. The brain can exist without consciousness, as for instance when a patient is in a coma, but consciousness cannot exist without the brain, despite the claims for immortality which have yet to be verified. The dependence would seem to be one way, and the mind a function of the brain.

To this very day, philosophers are primarily concerned with interior man, looking for the nature of reality in the essence of the self, where it just possibly may not be. But more about modern philosophy later.

If all this sounds like an awful lot to follow from the division between mind and matter which Descartes made, remember that he was the first to make it. It had never occurred to anyone before. I have allowed myself to get way ahead of the story in order to show you how enormous the results of a philosophical move can be.

The immediate effect of Descartes' philosophy was felt most by another philosopher whose name was Benedict de Spinoza. When Descartes died in 1650, Spinoza was only 18 years old. But quite early in his life he developed an independent spirit. He was a Jew but one who did not accept literally the Jewish teachings, and he said so in several books. The Jewish community in Amsterdam grew fearful that he would get them into trouble with the authorities, and so when he was only 24 he was formally read out of the Synagogue and the Jewish religion.

He took the news quite calmly and all his life behaved as a good Stoic should, though he never professed Stoicism. He remained indifferent to external events, ground lenses for a living, never married, and continued to write though not to publish. We learn from his letters that he refused the academic posts that were offered to him, preferring to remain in seclusion as the best way to preserve his independence, for he was by nature a non-joiner.

Looking back upon his work from the perspective of some centuries, we can see that he was not as independent as he himself had supposed. His independence was one of person but not of thought. He was influenced by the Jewish religion—and by Descartes' philosophy to a very large extent indeed. He used his own words to express his own philosophy, but if we look around them instead of at them, we can see the heavy shadow of Descartes falling across the page.

Spinoza, in fact, completed an important piece of scholarship before arriving at his own philosophy. Descartes had not presented his philosophy in the form of a system, and so Spinoza respectfully performed this task for him. We have still that version of Descartes' philosophy which was rewritten by Spinoza in order to present it as a system.

Spinoza treated his own ideas in much the same way. He used Euclid's geometry as a model this time, and tried to make almost a mathematically strict composition of his own system. He named this chief work *Ethics* because he thought that the end of thought lay in moral action. But there was a lot more to it than that.

The Jewish religion led him to insist upon the importance of God, who came back into his ideas as necessary to the explanation of reality. Everything was part of God, he said, but then his thought took a curious turn, for he added that God and nature are one and the same. "God or nature" was his phrase. *Nature* he understood to be the face of *God. God* was the One, *nature* the Many; they were simply different aspects of the same reality.

Both of course were infinite. Spinoza had another way of showing the infinite. Falling back upon Descartes' two classes of reality, *mind* and *matter,* Spinoza reminded us that the essence of mind is thought, meaning of course conscious thought, and the essence of matter is extension. Then he used a new word; he called *thought* and *extension attributes* of God (or nature), and assumed that while they were the only ones we recognized, still they were only two of an infinite number. God or nature has an infinity of attributes, of which we know only two: thought and extension.

According to Spinoza, *mind* and *body* work well together because what occurs in them is a parallel set of events. Everything that happens in one is the correspondent of something which happens in the other, but there is no interaction between them. Consciousness itself is "the idea of the body." Nothing is good or evil in itself, only in relation to human interests, but to God all things are fair. The emotions themselves are derived from the fundamental three feelings of desire, pleasure and pain. The emotions are the bodily equivalents of the mental ideas.

The good life for Spinoza was an intellectual life, freed from bondage to the emotions and devoted to God, "the intellectual love of God," he called it. Everything in nature must be accepted, Spinoza explained, because it comes from God. Not for nothing has Spinoza been described as a "God-intoxicated man"

—we would say rather, a man fascinated with an idea of God which was almost uniquely his own. For to no one before Bruno had God been equated with the whole of nature.

Spinoza's philosophy in one respect, however, was a step backward. For despite Descartes' piety, you will remember, he had left out *God* as a principle of explanation and depended only upon *mind* and *matter*. Spinoza put *God* back into the picture and endeavored to explain a lot in that way, the moral life for instance. But he did nothing to solve the dilemma which Descartes had bequeathed to philosophy. If *mind* and *matter* are so fundamental, what is the nature of their relationship?

The last of the philosophers on the mainland of western Europe to think he had solved that problem was the German, G. W. Leibniz. Leibniz was so original that it is not easy to see how he could not have been right. For he tried to explain the interaction between mind and body by bringing back the atoms of Democritus. He called them *monads*. Both mind and matter, he declared, are composed of millions of monads. Large size objects are only clusterings of monads.

But, he added, there is no interaction between them. Thus far he was in agreement with Spinoza. His part of the description was to compare both mind and matter to clocks. Suppose, he said, you had two clocks, keeping exactly the same time. You could note this and wonder if one was not the cause of the other, but this was not the case, because they were wound up together to keep the same time. Every monad is like a clock that was wound up from the beginning of its existence and contains everything that will ever happen to it. The winding up of the clocks by God Leibniz called *pre-established harmony*.

The unlikelihood of this theory is so strong that few since Leibniz have ever believed it. A wise man once said that problems in philosophy never get solved, they only get dropped. That is true in a sense, and it would be entirely true except for the fact that the problems are not only in philosophy, they are those of real life and therefore always exist. If you cannot understand the world as a division of mind and matter, either your division is wrong or you must pull back and attack the problem from another angle.

One more imaginative touch and one amusing story. If it is true, as Leibniz insisted, that the world was made out of millions of monads put together in a certain way, then there must be millions of possible worlds because there are millions of other ways in which the monads could be put together. And so, he said, there are. But, added Leibniz, perhaps to comfort us or himself, ours is the best of all possible worlds because while it contains evil it contains the least amount of evil necessary in order to have the greatest amount of good.

At this point a literary artist, satirist and professionally bitter man named Voltaire came into the picture. In a very short time he produced a parody of Leibniz' ideas, in a story called *Candide*. It has in its way been better known than the philosophy of Leibniz. In it, Voltaire made fun of the idea that this is the best of all possible worlds.

Several centuries later, an English philosopher named Bradley carried the joke one step further. Using the idea of Leibniz that some evil is always necessary, he described Leibniz' philosophy afresh and managed to make it sound like its own parody. "This is the best of all possible worlds," he declared, "and everything in it is a necessary evil."

One postscript to this chapter. Descartes was French, Spinoza Dutch, and Leibniz German. All lived on the continent of Europe, and all undertook to derive reliable knowledge from human reasoning alone. Hence the title by which they became known in the history of philosophy: *continental rationalists*. We shall have reason to refer to them again by this title.

Chapter IX

Knowledge from
Sense Experience Alone

The key problem in philosophy may here be stated again in Whitehead's words as discovering the answer to the question, "What is it all about?" The emphasis is on the word "all." Put it *all* together, the world, ourselves, everything, and then make as compact an explanation of it as possible. And that will be a philosophy. We have been looking at examples for some time and calling them *metaphysics*, because metaphysics tries to answer the question in terms of basic assumptions. In Greek the word meant originally "The works (of Aristotle) after the *Physics*." Because these works included the study of first principles, metaphysics came to be interpreted—or rather misinterpreted—as meaning the first principles beyond what is physical (or natural).

The briefest description of course would be the sentence, "All is one." That contains everything, alright. But as we have noted, the trouble with it is that it describes nothing. No single classification does because each puts everything in one bag. The next attempt therefore, while keeping the explanation as simple as possible would be to try two classes.

But which two? The *one-and-the-many? Permanence-and-*

change? The *universal-and-the-particular?* The *whole-and-its-parts? Mind-and-matter?*

We have seen all of these pairs tried. Take any one of the pairs without looking at the others and a strange thing happens to you. It is possible to become so bewitched by having to make a choice between the two you have selected that you don't notice you don't have to: after all, other pairs are possible. Besides, *reality* can be cut up in still other ways or be approached from quite another direction.

Let us look now, then, at one such approach made by the British philosophers. The scene in philosophy had moved to England, and in the seventeenth century was given a new direction by John Locke, who proposed to use *appearance-and-reality*. (You may recall that the early Greek philosopher, Parmenides, was the first one to use this division, though he did not employ it in quite the same way.)

Locke as a matter of fact kept another distinction he had inherited from Europe, the one between *mind-and-matter*. He wanted to know the relationship between them, just as his predecessors had. But because of the new interest in sense experience which the revival of science had aroused, he pursued that goal in terms of the method of acquiring knowledge, and he determined to pursue it exclusively in terms of sense experience. His theory of how knowledge is acquired was to be based on the sights we see, the sounds we hear, the odors we smell, the objects we touch, the food we taste. Chief among these, because it reaches out the farthest and takes in the most is the sense of sight.

This method was a new one in philosophy. Ever since the Greeks, men had wanted to know *what there is*. Now suddenly, as a result of the new interests awakened by science, men wanted to know *how we know* what there is. The new method was called *epistemology*, or the theory of knowledge. Curiously, "what there is" was reintroduced as a small part of the theory of knowledge. If you want to use the long words, philosophers now began to make epistemology central and to derive metaphysics from it. What we seek to *know* is of course *reality*. In the one case we are talking what we suppose to be the truth (metaphysics) and in the second case we occupy ourselves with inquiring how we know it to be true (epistemology).

The question Locke asked himself, and it was a comparatively new one, was: how can we know that the knowledge we have is reliable? By *mind* he of course meant the *conscious* mind, and for *matter* his phrase was *the external world*. How does the conscious mind know that the knowledge it obtains from the external world by means of sense experience is reliable? A thorny question indeed.

He began by assuming that the mind at birth is blank, a "clean slate" he said, on which nothing is written until the senses write. We can know reliably of nothing in the world except through the senses, with the single exception of God. Since Locke's proof of God's existence was the same as Descartes', we can ignore it here. It played no part in his system.

Relying on sense experience to tell him what lay outside, and employing his reasoning powers to put together what he had learned in this way, he obtained the following results. The objects in the external world consist primarily in something called *substance*. However, we never see or feel substance, all that we can see or feel are its qualities.

Locke recognized two quite different sorts of qualities, to which he gave the names *primary* and *secondary*. His *primary qualities* were what we could call the physical properties: for instance, *mass, density*, and the three *dimensions*. His *secondary qualities* are what we would call qualities, for instance, *sounds, colors, smells*, and *tastes*. You may remember that Democritus made the same distinction, but Locke added something that was peculiarly his own. He insisted that a material object is composed of a substance, to which are attached a number of primary and secondary qualities. We ourselves cannot perceive substance, only its qualities. And we see them equally, even though the primary qualities are permanently attached to the substance while the secondary qualities are what we ourselves have contributed to it.

Perhaps a picture might make that odd arrangement somewhat more understandable. Let us suppose for example that a man looks at a chair. The man, insisted Locke, does not see the *chair*, he cannot see substance, which he said is "something, we know not what," he sees only its *qualities*. He sees that it is four feet high, that it is three feet wide, that it weighs thirty pounds, that it is brown, and he can feel that it is made of a hard wood, etc.

He senses, in other words, only its *appearance*, not its *reality*. The "something, we know not what" is the reality behind the appearance, and Locke declared that it was unknowable, though he failed to tell us how he could know this much.

Let us look more closely at Locke's theory of sense perception because it will help us later. Speaking generally, he had a subject, the conscious mind; an object, the material thing, whatever it is; and a relation between them, or the act of perception. If we use a kind of shorthand, we can label the subject, "S," the material object, "O," and the relation between them, "R." The knowledge relation then will look something like this: S (subject) $- R$ (relation) $- O$ (object).

That of course does not describe exactly what Locke said. For Locke had eliminated the object from reliable knowledge. According to him we have no sense experience of it as it is in itself. As a "substance," and to be a part of reliable knowledge, remember, it has to be sensed in some way. Locke's modification of the theory of knowledge would therefore look more like this: $S - R -$ and not O but in its place selected primary and secondary qualities.

In other words, Locke thought that we can sense the qualities which are attached to the object of knowledge, both those that belong to it—the primary qualities—and those we contribute ourselves—the secondary qualities—but *not* the object itself.

Locke, in short, had got rid of the object. He did not mean that to stop us from referring our knowledge to a substance, for substance is for him the basis of everything in the external world. But it did mean that we must refer knowledge to something which is permanently unknowable.

A curious arrangement, no? A man knows there is a stable element in the external world but knows also that he cannot know it and that he must therefore remain confined to his own sense perceptions, limited except for the primary qualities to sensing only what he himself sends out into the world? Curious, but that *is* what Locke said.

He said a great many more things than that, but that was his main point. He said also that since absolute knowledge of the object was impossible to obtain, we would all have to get along on probabilities. Here he was repeating what the Greek Skeptics had maintained. And there he was on to something. For it is true enough of course that our actions are guided by probabilities. We do those things which we judge have a pretty good chance of succeeding and usually we do not "take foolish chances."

Locke had something else to add, and that was an idea which much later came to be called "wishful thinking," the tendency people have to believe that what they *wish* to be true *is* true.

He said that *infinity* and *power* are negative ideas, not things experienced in themselves, but the results of what we experience. He thought the same of *cause-and-effect*, that we do not directly experience any such thing. The same fate met the old idea of *universals*. We experience *resemblances* between things and we call those resemblances "universals" but we have no experience of universals.

The story of Locke's philosophy would not be complete without an account of his political theories. Like most of us he lived through a series of wars, and like some of us he felt obliged to consider a solution theoretically. The years of the wars, which are known collectively as the "Thirty Years' War" (1618-1648) overlapped those of his own life (1632-1704).

The bloodless Revolution of 1688, which was settled by the Bill of Rights after William of Orange had been invited back to England to assume the throne in place of James II, decided in favor of Protestantism over Catholicism, but it also established the principle of universal toleration and the practical separation of church and state, and it protected the individual in his rights.

Locke's political theory was a perfect reflection of these events. He wrote *Two Treatises on Government* and three letters *Concerning Toleration* in which he gathered together all of the threads of the common sense of the time and passed on to the future western democracies their most important justification.

For Locke the "state of nature is one of peace, good will, mutual assistance and preservation." In this he was opposed to Hobbes' idea that each man was perpetually at war with every other man. Civil society derives from the consent of its members the right to make laws having penalties involving the preservation of property for the public good. Government, affirmed Locke, is nothing except the natural power of each man resigned "into the hands of the community," and is conducted therefore only with the consent of the governed. It is responsible to the members of the community which it governs, and its powers are limited both by the moral law which prevails and by constitutional traditions.

Its aim is the defense of individual liberty and property— Locke's phrase was "life, liberty, and estate." Property is a natural right of the individual since it exists prior to society. By his labor and energy the individual makes it a part of himself. Within the government the legislative branch is more important, more authoritative, than the executive, and there is a strict separation to be preserved between them.

Let us return now to pick up the threads of the development of the theory of knowledge which we were pursuing when I interrupted the flow to talk about Locke's political theory. The Greek philosophers had one great advantage. The life of the city-state was a small world which made it quite easy to see it steadily and as a whole. That advantage no longer exists, and so the philosopher has been compelled to consider one enterprise at a time, often neglecting the obvious fact that no matter how complex human institutions become, they *are* all connected.

The next thinker in the succession of those who developed knowledge theory was named George Berkeley. Berkeley had read Locke. Also, he was a Bishop in the Anglican Church. And so he revised Locke's theory of how reliable knowledge is obtained by taking what must have appeared to be the next logical step, but he also brought God back into the explanation.

How can knowledge be a product of the relations between subject and object when there is no knowable object? The argument is impossible to answer if you accept Locke's position. Accordingly, Berkeley got rid of the relation of knowledge. Berkeley's picture of the knowledge relation looked something like this. S —, where both the R and the O had been eliminated.

The move left him with a problem, however. If there is no object, what happens to the primary and secondary qualities? The primary qualities belonged to the object, remember, but the secondary qualities, the sense qualities, presented no difficulty because they already belonged to the subject and had simply been borrowed by the object.

Berkeley's solution to the problem was a sweeping one. He declared that all qualities, primary as well as secondary, belong to the subject. What exists, then, is what the subject perceives with his senses, no more and no less. In what has become a famous principle, he declared that "to be is to be perceived." What is not perceived just does not exist.

If there is no substance in the world, according to Berkeley, then of course neither can there be any in man. What is real in man is the spirit of man, as you might expect a Bishop to suppose, a spirit which, as usual, is left undescribed. And the spirit of man is somehow also his consciousness, the area in which the sense qualities exist.

So far, so good. But, as usual, simple answers often leave complex questions behind them. Do you mean to say, his opponents asked him, that when I leave the room and can no longer observe what is in it, that nothing is there? If a tree is struck by lightning in a dense forest and crashes to the ground, can you say that it makes no noise if there is no one to hear it? Do the distant stars cease to exist in the daytime when I no longer see them?

What looked like very tough questions turned out to be easy for the good Bishop to answer, because he had a forgotten card up his sleeve. There was still the condition that any answer he made had to be in terms of sense perception, for that was the rule of the game that, following Locke, he had decided to play. The answer was easy because Berkeley had simply to appeal to God. The reason why things exist when I don't perceive them, he said, is because God perceives them. The furniture in the room, the tree in the forest, the stars in the sky, all exist as they do because God continually perceives them.

What about matter, then? You can sort of tell in advance what his answer would have to be. Matter is no more than a collection of sense qualities, and when we speak of any material thing what we have in mind is a vague image of some particular example of it. When we think of a cup what we have is the image of some cup we have handled, for there is no general class of cups or of anything else. No universals exist as such, only particulars.

Berkeley was an *idealist,* that is one who thought that reality is of the nature of mind, a set of ideas and nothing more. And he was a *nominalist* in believing that *universals* or absolutely general classes do not exist, they are merely names. Only material particulars exist, though he reduced even them to the ideas of them in the mind.

Bishop Berkeley at last had his theory of reliable knowledge. What is real, he concluded, is the spirit of man together with the sensed qualities of his mind—the human spirit together with God, and such sense experiences as they both may have. The sense experiences which man has were imparted to him by God, who perceives him as well.

The next, and last, of the three great British philosophers who relied upon sense experience alone for the reliable knowledge of reality was David Hume. We ordinarily think of Hume as the latter-day inheritor of Greek Skepticism, and so he was. The first thing he doubted was philosophy itself as it had usually been presented.

He was most vigorous in following the principle adopted by his predecessors, Locke and Berkeley: that nothing should be accepted as knowledge unless it had been acquired through sense experience. He thought it a good principle to go on, but accused them of violating it themselves.

For instance, in the knowledge relation with which they had all started, $S - R - O$, Locke had got rid of the object, O, but had kept the relation, R, and the subject, S. Berkeley had improved on this somewhat. He had got rid of the object, O and the relation R, but had kept the subject S.

Now Hume made an even more radical proposal. He proposed to get rid of the subject, S, as well!

He had a good reason for taking such a step. He said: if we are relying entirely upon sense experience, then there is no experience of the subject or self. You do not have any experience of your self. You may experience sense impressions, you may even experience your own ideas. But the self as such, all by itself, you do not experience.

He was right, of course; we don't.

What then is left to experience? Nothing at all?

Not so, he replied. We have left the *contents* of experience. What we experience as a matter of fact is not the object, not the subject and not the relations between them. We experience our own sense impressions and we experience our own ideas. These occur one after the other in an endless train so long as we are in the waking state. The *impressions* are of course sense impressions and they are primary. The *ideas* are derived from the impressions by association with memories of similar impressions. They don't stand by themselves but are thus shown to be merely big blocks of impressions. There would be no such thing as abstract *universals*. The only difference between impressions and ideas, he insisted, is that "impressions" are more lively, more vivid, than "ideas," because more immediate and less dependent on memory.

Thus, in his view and relying entirely upon sense experience, we cannot be sure of the existence either of a self or of an external world, only of a succession of impressions and ideas which flow through our consciousness.

Hume was not satisfied to have destroyed our beliefs in an external world and in ourselves. He went on to knock down some of the more common ideas which we have all accepted.

All that we have left to go on, he insisted, are relations among ideas and matters of fact. The relations of ideas are limited by what relations there could be, and that is not an infinite number by any means. The matters of fact are not connected by cause-and-effect, as had been supposed. Hume was able to disprove the connection between cause-and-effect, in so far as it was based on perception. "One thing may cause another," he said, "but if so you cannot rest your beliefs on what you perceive."

Watch me as I push the book off the table. What do you see? he asked.

I see you push the book off the table, I reply.

You see no such thing, he insisted. You may think that is what I am doing from what you see, but you don't see me do it. What you actually see if you stick to the sense of sight is my hand and the book moving closely together toward the edge of the table until the book moves over the edge and down toward the floor while my hand comes to a stop. That is what you see and no more. The rest is what you infer from what you already knew.

Hume repeated many of the arguments of the Greek Skeptics, arguments which had been conveniently forgotten but never answered. The belief in cause-and-effect was demolished, as we have just seen. So was the belief in God, in an argument which Hume took over from the Stoics. It runs somewhat as follows.

There is evil in the world, nobody denies that. Moreover, we cannot imagine a God who is not both all good and all powerful. But how can such a God be reconciled with the fact of evil? For if God were all good He would want to abolish evil, and if He were all powerful He would be able to do so. Since there is evil in the world, His existence is in doubt.

Hume's radical position led him to reject all previous philosophies. He swept away the basis of all our beliefs, but since all actions follow from beliefs how can we act? Hume had his answer ready for this question, too. We act as we always have acted and as those who have gone before us have acted: from custom and tradition. That means of course acting without the certainty that our actions are the right ones.

As for the philosophy books, he said, ask yourself the following question. Do they contain any abstract reasoning concerning number or experimental reasoning concerning matters of fact? If the answer is, No, then commit them to the flames, for they contain nothing but illusion.

Book-burners have usually been politicians or mobs led by them. Only too often when Roman Catholic priests have accompanied the invaders of primitive countries, such as the early Mexican civilizations of the Aztecs and Mayans, they saw to it that all non-Christian books were burned. The Nazis of course were fond of book-burnings. But Hume was one of the first philosophers ever to advise such a course of action.

Philosophers, as a rule have not been as innocent as I have made them seem to be by singling out Hume as the first intolerant one. Intolerance is the rule among philosophers, not the exception. They have never thought that those who differed with them should be allowed to express their views. On the contrary, they have been an easy prey to politicians who wished to make their own positions official and absolute.

The intolerance is with us still today. There are always exceptions but the exceptions are rare. By and large, when philosophers of a particular viewpoint capture a department of philosophy in a university, they refuse to hire anyone who does not agree with them. They are unwilling to grant freedom—and jobs—to those who hold different views.

Hume was a convinced Skeptic and a pretty hard man to prove wrong. There is one tiny passage, however, in which he let the air in and gave his opponents an opportunity to reject his teachings.

He could explain everything but action. Since "action and the occupations of common life" are designed to change things in the external world, they do seem to suggest that such an external world exists. By the use of action, he admitted, Skepticism could be undermined. An illustration is easy to find. If you agree with Berkeley and Hume that matter as such does not exist, try walking through a table rather than around it. Samuel Johnson showed Berkeley that the reality of the external world could be demonstrated by kicking a stone.

This is not to say, however, that Skepticism does not have its uses. If you examine the basis for your beliefs, as so many philosophers from the Greek Skeptics to Descartes and Hume have advised, you will end either by rejecting them yourself or by finding a firmer basis for them, and in either case you will probably be better off. Skepticism is a useful ingredient in the process of arriving at reliable knowledge, but it is not that knowledge itself.

We may pause at this point in order to see what the three philosophers we have just been studying had in common. As we have already noted, they had a common reliance on sense experience to give them reliable knowledge. Those who behave in this way are called *empiricists* and their method is called *empiricism*, a fancy word for sense experience and the knowledge derived exclusively from it. Locke, Berkeley and Hume were as it happened all British, hence the term "British empiricism."

Chapter X

The Triumph of Science

When we look over the range of history, we note broad and distinct movements like giant waves in human society. If they seem to be the effects of sudden developments, it is because we can look back so many hundreds of years behind them. The Middle Ages was certainly a period when religion was uppermost, and we date it roughly from the fourth to the fourteenth centuries. That was a thousand years, a long time in human life. But the influence of religion in western Europe did not begin or stop abruptly. It was a long time building and an equally long time declining.

Do you remember that I tried to show how the relative importance culturally of Nature, God and Man had changed from Greece to the Middle Ages? Well, for the age of science the relative proportions changed again.

Nature is central once more, as it was for the Greeks. Man has increased slightly in size, but God is small again and this time outside the picture. God is still considered supernatural, as He was in the Middle Ages, but of relatively lesser importance because His existence was not susceptible of investigation.

Apart from the professional philosophers, the ideas which were current in the sixteenth century were marked by inclusiveness rather than by consistency. Alternately Skeptics and believers, Stoics and Epicureans—both Montaigne and Shakespeare for instance—liked to savor opposite viewpoints and to feel the qualities of them. Not too much was known at the time about physical nature—that was to come later—but these men knew a very great deal about that part of nature which we have come to call "human nature," so comprehensive in its diversity, and with all of its faults and virtues, its courage and cowardice, its pretensions and confessions, its boasts and its self-pity, its cruelty and its kindness, its trust in events, its moral reserve.

Science appeared rather abruptly on the scene. When Galileo made and looked through the first telescope, the Church was still strong enough to compel him to say that he had not seen what in fact he knew he had seen. It is difficult to remember now that the year Galileo died Isaac Newton was born! That year, 1642, ought to be known as the year when science took a giant leap forward. Galileo had not been alone. There had been Kepler in astronomy, Gilbert in electric phenomena, Gesner in zoology, Vesalius in medicine and anatomy. But the work of Newton represented a new kind of consolidation, and Newtonian mechanics prevailed for some time. By the end of the seventeenth century the scientific movement, which was to accelerate so rapidly that it transformed men's lives and even changed the face of the earth, was fully launched. It was not so long a time, then, from the scientific work of the monks and others, of Robert Grosseteste in the fourteenth century, say, and of Francis Bacon in the fifteenth, to the achievements of the scientists of Newton's day.

The scientific movement as a social movement, one which was to influence everything in human life, from the practice of medicine to the developments of new forms of power in peace and war, took a long while to get going. What it chiefly introduced, and that at its outset, was a new method of inquiry. Briefly, the scientific method can be described as a method of finding the laws of nature by making observations with instruments leading to guesses, called hypotheses, which are then tested by means of experiments and mathematical calculations.

The scientific method has been responsible for turning up all sorts of facts, many of a new and puzzling kind. But its aim, and its chief accomplishment, has been the discovery of the laws which phenomena obey. This has given men not only an understanding of the world but also a large measure of control over it. Important to its understanding is the Platonic nature of its laws. They seem to belong to the class of abstract universals. For the first time men were no longer dependent upon pure thought to support the belief in such universals but they could find substantiating evidence in the material world. The law of gravitation to which all material bodies conform does seem to be more durable than the bodies which attract each other in the fixed way which that law describes so accurately.

Most people do not appreciate the extent to which the common sense they live by was constructed for them years before. Its authors were the philosophers and physicists who put together the kind of world-view on which such common sense depends.

For instance, ever since the seventeenth century the ideas of the makers of the modern world—Descartes, Locke and Newton—have prevailed. Descartes separated mind from matter, while Locke and Newton told us what kind of matter it was. They said it consisted in static and rigid bodies in uniform motion in space and time with physical dimensions, but lacking qualities until human sense perceptions put them there. They said it was in continual motion, and that the motions were governed by the laws of gravitation. Together these ideas, and some other ones closely related, constituted a coherent scheme which underlay what everyone in the western world came implicitly to believe without ever understanding its source.

The scientific method was so powerful that it took the place of other kinds of investigation. The philosophers felt its power most of all. They reacted in one of two ways. Either they said:

surrender to science and give up such useless pursuits as the search for reality, because if there is any such thing science will find it. Or they said: since science has taken over the external world and will tell us all about the object of knowledge, we are left therefore no choice but to withdraw into the subject.

This last alternative was by far the most popular among the philosophers, so popular in fact that I am going to give it a special name. I am going to call it the *subjective by-pass*. I am going to call it that because it meant going around the consideration of the world with all of its richness and variety, skirting it, so to speak, in order to get back the sooner to a concentration on the self.

As we shall see in the remainder of this book, it was not necessary either to surrender to science or to retreat into the subject. Both choices, as I hope to show, were dead ends for philosophy.

First, let us look at the surrender to science.

The philosophy which advocated this step is called *positivism*. Briefly it called for giving up philosophy, if by philosophy is meant metaphysics, and instead insisted on pointing with pride to science. But the world still needs metaphysics, if for no other reason than in order to understand the position of science among the other disciplines. As to pointing with pride, that should be left to the scientists themselves.

Secondly, let us look at the retreat into the subject.

Philosophy in taking a subjective by-pass ran into a blind alley. The decision to follow that road was a momentous one, and in my opinion a wrong one, but it does have so many turns and by-ways that it is sometimes hard to see how it could always be the same road. Consider the following: states of awareness, the organization of thought and thought processes, and the will. What they all have in common is that they share a place in the subject. The subjective by-pass as we conceive it in the west leads nowhere and in any case is outdone by the ancient Asian religions and the current Asian religious practices. If you want to retreat into the self, Hinduism is the best guide.

If we go back a little we can see quite easily how the philosophers got themselves into such a pickle. Let us return to the rise of *empiricism*, the doctrine that sense experience is the only source of reliable knowledge. We can trace the following confusion back to a different understanding of the term *empiricism* on the part of the scientists and philosophers. When the eighteenth century *scientists* used the word "empiricism," they meant *what* they experienced. When the *philosophers* of that period used the same word, they meant *how they* experienced.

A whole world lay between the two points of view. It separated the scientists and philosophers for the first time in the history of philosophy, and sent them off in opposite directions. For the scientists were led to the experimental method of learning about nature, while the philosophers were led only to learning about themselves. The scientific method produced an abundant and diverse knowledge of new facts and laws. The philosophical method produced only a monotonous account of private perceptions and sensations.

Let me see if I can make this clear by means of a simple example. An ornithologist watching a colony of seagulls would find many similarities and differences, while a philosopher watching the same animals would find only a view of his own internal reactions. The ornithologist might end by establishing some laws which hold true for the science of zoology. The philosopher would end by knowing more about his own processes of sense perception which further such investigations would not add to.

Sense experience, as you may remember from reading earlier about the ideas of Locke, Berkeley and Hume, who began to examine it, is a tricky term. It can mean *the act of experience* or it can mean *what is experienced*. They are not the same thing. Do you remember the description of sense experience, with a subject, *S*, having the experience, a material object, *O*, which is experienced, and a relation, *R*, between them?

You can perhaps see now that there would be a great deal of confusion in trying to determine how this operates. Just where does the "experience" of sense experience enter into the picture? Is it something the *object* causes? After all, there would be no experience unless there was something to be experienced. Is it something that occurs in a *subject*? Surely, if there was no one to have the experience there could be no experience. Or is it neither the subject nor the object alone but something that happens when they are brought together? Certainly it does have to involve a *relation* between them.

The result of the introduction of the new scientific method, which laid as much claim to sense experience as the early philosophers did, was not inevitable. Nevertheless, the scientists went one way, and the philosophers another, both claiming to be *empiricists*. The scientists with their laboratory procedure, their instruments and their mathematical measurements, took the object of knowledge to be their province and gave us more information about the external world than we had ever had before. The philosophers understood this scientific achievement to mean that it left them only with the subject of knowledge. And so from the seventeenth century onward, that is what they proceeded to investigate.

The contrast between the philosophers and the experimental scientists, both of whom counted themselves empiricists, is a sharp one. While Descartes was trying to free his mind of all preconceptions and to make a fresh start in belief with the *cogito, ergo sum* (I think, therefore I am) as a beginning, Galileo was inventing the telescope and with it finding evidence for the Copernican system. While Spinoza was trying to work out by means of reason alone the modifications of substance, Boyle was conducting experiments which led to the discovery that if the temperature of a gas is constant, the pressure is proportional to the density. And while Leibniz was trying to invoke God in aid of his principle of pre-established harmony, Newton was occupied in establishing by means of the prism that lights of different colors were all contained in white light.

It is a long story, and perhaps we have not come to the end of it yet. But the turn taken by philosophers in the seventeenth and eighteenth centuries was an error, because it shut them out from the largest part of reality. The interest of the philosophers turned inward rather than outward. Leaving the study of the vast external world to the care of the scientists, they decided to concentrate on the internal world of the mind. But this was to make a detour around the world and to neglect it almost altogether.

A little detachment might have told the philosophers that the world is *not* part of the human mind, but instead the human mind *is* part of the world. The world may be reflected in the mind but does not owe its existence to the mind. You would not think that the best place to study anything would be in its reflection, anymore than a man should be studied in a mirror. That was not the only way philosophy could have gone, that is not the way it will always go, but that was the way it went from that day to our own. That is the way it is still going. We shall see that there have been exceptions, but for the most part philosophers thenceforth investigated the self, conscious thought, and other aspects of the human subject, such as his intentions and his knowledge of other minds.

One distressing result was that the philosophers did not want to be literary physicists and so they became instead amateur psychologists. Their efforts to escape from the influence of science was a failure. I hope to show you before we are done that there are other ways philosophy can go, and in fact, as you will see, there are other ways philosophy has gone. Some philosophers *have* managed to take account of the findings of the sciences without losing their own identity, and they are the bigger for it.

Between the decline of one great period in history and the rise of another, there often appear thinkers who face both ways: toward what is fading into the past and toward what is coming in the future. One such thinker was Descartes in the seventeenth century, and another was Giovanni Battista Vico in the eighteenth. Vico was not a rounded philosopher, like the great Greek ones we have looked at, and his influence, while not as immense as Descartes', was still considerable because he worked in a field in which not much had been done before him (except by Ibn Khaldûn in the fourteenth century, a lonely and isolated figure indeed). That field was the philosophy of history.

History itself may be described as an account of civilizations and of the ways in which they rise and fall. The *philosophy* of history is an attempt to find out what makes them do so.

Vico's theory was that history has a certain shape. There is, he thought, a sort of standing structure to history, one which repeats itself over and over. History falls for him into three well-marked periods, to which he gave names and descriptions. They are stages in an "ideal eternal history" which has its course laid out in time.

The first stage is that of primitive man. There was once, he said, a race of giants living in a state of nature, without tools or artifacts of any kind. We can see traces of them still if we examine folk poetry and common superstitions. This stage was characterized by a sacred language, and by necessity and utility.

The next stage is that of heroic man. He practiced only the stern virtues. He was cruel, combative, and self-disciplined. All of his morality was based on force in the hands of the stronger. He lived in small communities and employed a poetic and symbolic language. We can read at least one account of heroic man in the epics of Homer. This stage was characterized by comfort and pleasure.

The last stage for Vico is that of civilized man. It was much as we know it today, a civil society made by man himself, with man-made laws. It was ruled, so far as Vico could see in the eighteenth century, by a limited monarchy, characterized by luxury and waste, and employed the language of the common people. Although it was rational, like the others it was destined not to last.

History, in other words, he insisted, has no outcome. It is dominated by a repetition of occurrences. There is an eternal return of the cycle. After the present third stage, there will recur a new first stage. Humanity itself is divine, though there is no especially divine human. Humanity in recognizing its own history accepts and reckons with its own achievement.

Vico taught the world that history—human social history—was not a mystery to be referred to God by way of explanation but was instead the work of man himself and had its own structure and its own laws that could be discovered just like the laws of the physical world. Vico was perhaps the first to understand that the entire sweep of history could be caught up and described with more or less accuracy in a single comprehensive and widely self-consistent scheme in which all actual societies were determined by their possibilities in a way which still left some freedom to the individual. We are a long way from the establishment of social science, but Vico was the first to see how it could be brought about.

He was the forerunner of what was to become a tradition of philosophers of history. Although ordinarily they are not included in the roster of philosophers, that is where they belong. I have in mind the much neglected Russian, Nicolai Danilevsky in the nineteenth century and, in our own century, Oswald Spengler and Arnold Toynbee.

While Vico was studying civilizations, another man was criticizing them. We, living today in the midst of so many of the products of applied science and technology, and benefitting from so many developments that we cannot ourselves understand, such as antibiotics and television, to name but two, are well aware that we have lost the kind of simple life our remote ancestors enjoyed.

"Enjoyed" is the right word. Jean-Jacques Rousseau, the French philosopher who lived in the eighteenth century, insisted that human life had been spoiled by civilization. He compared civilized man with primitive man and found primitive man better in all aspects. The "noble savage" is not only happier but less degraded than civilized man, he declared. In primitive societies, he mistakenly thought, all men are equal and private property is unknown. In civilization, the arts as well as the sciences are corrupting influences. They lead to luxury which undermines all of the simple virtues, and they lead to social inequalities.

By contrast Rousseau painted an attractive picture of the "noble savage" living in a "state of nature," social and peace-loving and full of sympathy for his fellow man. Without the constraining influence of family life and without the evil influence of government, he can live in the idyllic state that follows from a life of romantic love, free of all selfishness and possessiveness.

Unfortunately, no such happy and noble savage as Rousseau had in mind has ever been found. Probably none exists. It was a product of his imagination. Thanks to missionaries, explorers and anthropologists, we know a great deal more about primitive societies all over the globe than was known in Rousseau's day, and we have found few to correspond to his description. I myself once cherished the view that the natives of Tahiti before the arrival of the white man had lived paradisaical lives of simplicity, leisure and love-making. That was some years before I learned that they had fought wars and practiced cannibalism! So much for that dream. The bitter truth is that although some primitive peoples have many virtues, many for the most part are dirty, diseased, ignorant, short-lived and war-like.

Rousseau did see that some kind of political arrangement is necessary and he found that he liked Hobbes' idea of a commonwealth freely entered into by the individual but without surrendering political power, which must continue to remain with him. His idea was that society is founded on a "social contract" made by people through laws which they freely impose on themselves and which express the general will, the "will of all," in which each individual wills the common good. He wanted government to exist only so long as it had the consent of those it governed. This idea eventually became a cornerstone of democracy, however much it has been violated.

Rousseau also had some good ideas about education, which could always use them. He suggested that the child should be led into learning rather than forced into it, and allowed to develop along its own lines and in its own way. He wanted education to be not artificial but as natural as possible. He saw it as a development of capacities rather than as an imposition of ideas, nurtured by love and understanding, not by compulsion. He thought it would be best to employ the naturally good impulses of the child, and not have to present knowledge as hedged about by duties, obligations and commands. Children ought to learn by imitating their parents, but it was the parents' virtues that he had in mind, not their vices.

So far, so good. Education had been, and was to become again for a while, a form of child torture. It ought to be a happy period in the child's life, not one of utter misery. But Rousseau went too far. He wanted to prepare the child to be a happy savage, not a civilized man. And so his version of education was to prevent all formal education in order to allow the natural virtues to develop by themselves, such virtues as goodness, courage, and honesty. There was to be no information, and indeed no knowledge. And so alas for the child when it became an adult, no future.

The spirit of innovation, which motivated Rousseau, had in fact been around for quite some time. The decline of religion and the rise of science was a period in which many new ideas were being introduced at the expense of the old. You cannot try out new developments unless there has been some reason to doubt the old customs and institutions. Skepticism, in other words, is a necessary pivot.

Michel de Montaigne, who had wondered in his rambling essays whether he could know anything with any degree of certainty, lived at the end of the sixteenth century. The Skepticism of the seventeenth century was replaced by new discoveries in the eighteenth and nineteenth. In these two hundred years doubt became as familiar as belief.

They were exciting periods, in which new horizons were being opened up and new institutions founded at an amazing rate, ideas and inventions which would affect the future of

Europe and its satellite countries for centuries to come. Among these we may count individualism, humanism, science, democracy, capitalism and the beginnings of business and manufacture, the exploration of the new world of the Americas, and the rise of Protestant Christianity.

Let us take a little time here to look more closely at these new movements. One of them, science, I have already described at the beginning of this chapter. The others belong together in groups. For instance, we can talk about humanism, individualism, and Protestantism together. And, similarly, we can talk about capitalism, industrialism and exploration together.

Briefly, humanism is the philosophy which states that the condition of man, individual man himself as he is here and now, should be his prime concern, and that human values should be preferred to all others. By "human values" were meant of course the positive values, not the negative. Pain and suffering should be eliminated, and individual self-development encouraged. To do unto others as you would have them do unto you, so long advocated, was now about to be practiced.

Unfortunately, such practice was always strictly limited. It applied only to "our kind," it did not apply to the natives the European explorers of North and South America encountered. And there were many other places, closer to home, where it did not apply. Humanism was not the philosophy of the Roman Catholic Christians when the new Protestant religions appeared in their midst. We have already noted that the wars of religion in Europe in the sixteenth century were as savage and brutal as any wars that had ever been fought.

Here of late, to get somewhat ahead of our story, the Europeans and Americans have been treated to the spectacle of an Asian culture which had never been guided by humanism but had always accepted pain as a part of human life. The Asians evidently enjoy pain in others, and are not too surprised when those others enjoy it in them. The deliberate torture of political prisoners is all of the evidence we need. But the truth is that the

Asian countries, the Soviet Union, China and their satellites, count life as cheap and do not value each and every individual, as we who have lived under humanism do. We have our lapses, but theirs are not lapses because they do not subscribe to the doctrine of humanism in the first place. Starvation, genocide even, are not unusual nor regarded with horror, as they are in the west. The German Nazis notwithstanding, this is not in general the approved western way of life.

The first principle of Protestant Christianity was that individual man should seek to communicate with God directly and does not need the mediation of a church or of a clergy. The Protestant churches therefore tended to be gatherings of worshippers guided by ministers. The word "Protestant" has misled many into thinking that it was a negative protest merely against certain practices and beliefs of the Roman Catholic religion. It was that, too, but it had its own positive program.

Both humanism and Protestantism were inspired by individualism, the theory that the individual should be the first consideration, not society and not any institution, including the institution of the Catholic Church. Representative democracy, in which every individual citizen votes for those who he thinks will vote for his good, was of course an outcome of the same movement.

Capitalism, the use of money to further economic enterprises from which the capitalist himself would gain the most benefits, arose at this time also. No other system would have made possible the invention and use of the factory to replace cottage industry. The emergence of the need for new markets and for raw materials was related to the new spirit of exploration. The world was wide, and much of it was being discovered for the first time.

The Scandinavians had been coming in their little boats around the great circle touching Iceland, Greenland, Labrador, and Nova Scotia on their way to what is now called the United States, long before Columbus and his men officially got the credit for the discovery of "the new world." The Vikings followed much the same route that is now employed by the jumbo jets, the Boeing 747s, when they fly from London to New York.

All of these modern developments, we may note significantly, were the work of the middle class, the "burghers," those new inhabitants who came up in the towns and cities to replace the monarchy, the land-holding aristocracy, the clergy and the farmers. It is fashionable nowadays to make fun of the middle class, but the middle class was responsible for most of what is good in the modern world, and the communists, those staunch advocates of the laboring class, admire and imitate middle-class achievements.

Just look at the benefits we owe to the burghers. I will mention only a few. Modern medicine with its hospitals, its surgical techniques and its drugs. Democratic government, with its divided interest-groups and its ability to survive peaceful change. Modern industrial productivity, which has produced not only a wealth of consumer goods but also enough wheat in the central plains of the United States to feed their two hundred million citizens, to say nothing of those of the Soviet Union and some of those of Communist China, countries which were in 1972 and 1973 unable to feed themselves. The modern period has witnessed a rapid and enormous increase in population all over the world which would not until much later manage to provide the basic needs: food, shelter, clothing and medical attention in the undeveloped countries.

Many of the new benefits were the result of the discoveries of the pure sciences and of their applications by means of the applied sciences and technology, the triumphs of the scientific-industrial, middle-class culture. Despite the enormous material benefits, many still feel that something has been lacking. With the decline of belief in the traditional religions, there has been a lack in what for want of a better word we may with some misgivings call the "spiritual values." The developments of abstract and non-representative forms in all of the fine arts reflect rather than relieve this feeling.

Philosophy might have stepped into the breach, but it did not, for this was the period also when, alas, the philosophers took off into their own private worlds, and had no strong influence on social events. But that is somewhat ahead of our story.

Chapter XI

The Greatest
European Philosophers I

The theory of knowledge continued to dominate philosophy throughout the 18th century. It was a century when the horizons of Europe were greatly widened. Europeans extended their interests and their domination over a large part of the world. Wars were of course, as usual, heavily involved. The Europeans fought not only at home now but also abroad. Traders as well as the military were the chosen instruments, and as often as not they were combined. The Spanish had begun much earlier. They were interested in religion and the search for gold, but they ended up by settling for trading posts. A South and Central America largely Spanish was the result. The English conquered India by means of a commercial venture, the East India Company, which had begun by doing business in the coastal towns but ended by dominating the whole of India, after winning a war there with the French. In 1858 the Crown took over and India became a British colony. The French and British also fought over North America, with the British again winning.

To all of this the philosophers turned a deaf ear. Instead of asking themselves, "What is this vast world like and what can we learn from it?" they were inclined to say, instead, "The only part of the world which interests me is the part I can know." More special still, instead of saying "That part of the world which comes to me through my experience is the part that interests me" they were apt to say "That part of the world which comes to me through my experience is to me the only part." In short, it was not the world which occupied the attention of the philosophers but that small part of it which they experienced.

The interest of philosophers was exclusively in the nature of mind, an interest which I have named "the subjective by-pass," and it now went around many brutal and forceful but significant events, of the kind which as a matter of fact usually do dominate the external world. Yet the philosophers while ignoring these developments still managed to produce some pretty tall figures.

Chief of the thinkers who took this road in the eighteenth century was Immanuel Kant, a descendant of Scotch parents who lived in Germany where he was born. I call him the chief because he tried to make a comprehensive system of philosophy in which reality hung upon knowing. There has to be a certain reality in order for us to know it, was his contention, and so he made reality subordinate to knowing.

Remember what he had to call on: the reasonings of the Continental rationalists, Descartes, Spinoza and Leibniz, and the theories of sense experience of the British empiricists, Locke, Berkeley and Hume. He had also the metaphysical classifications of all the previous philosophers we have read about. By skillful selection he was able to put them together in a way which made them fit and moreover made them his own. He did this in a way I propose to show you presently.

But first I have to prepare the ground a little. Nobody had ever associated the findings of the rationalists and the empiricists. That was bound to make a difference because Kant had to find out some system in which they would be consistent. Then too there was another very important point. What I have called just above "the classifications of the previous philosophers" were their divisions of reality. You remember what they were: *permanence-and-change, the one-and-the-many, appearance-and-reality, possibility, impossibility, quantity* and *quality*, etc. Well, these were metaphysical classifications because they were the underlying descriptions of reality. Kant called them *categories*. If now Kant meant to put such very different ideas together in a single system, he would have to go beyond what any one who wrote about them had believed. He would have to build each category into a theory of knowledge as an essential part of it, thus making his theory of reality, his metaphysics, a subordinate part of his epistemology. As a consequence the metaphysics almost got lost and his philosophy became one vast epistemological scheme.

One key to Kant's philosophy is that he saw all of it as hung on experience, conscious and deliberate experience. The universal ideas which were not products of experience could still be linked to it by calling them *a priori*, because they came before experience. The rest was *a posteriori*, or after experience. That put everything, both the abstract ideas which we have and the sense data we encounter, in direct relation to experience.

Kant drew on Locke's work for the justification to assert the final unknowability of the outer object of knowledge, the material thing. And he drew on Hume's conclusions to assert also the final unknowability of the inner subject, the "self." The former he called the *phenomena*, literally that which appears to consciousness, the latter he called the *noumena*, which was the unknowable self. The conscious mind, in the very act of knowing through sense experience, pulls all this together though it has no way of being sure that what it experiences corresponds to reality. Kant finally must have supposed, I think, that what appears to the human mind in experience *is itself* the reality.

Let us go back to the diagram of sense experience by means of which we were able to see what Locke, Berkeley and Hume had meant by it, the subject having the experience, the object experienced and the experience of the relation between them, $S - R - O$.

With Kant, there are some other unique features to note immediately. For instance, the relationship, *R*, has been greatly enriched. It now carries *all* of the possible theories of reality. Also, it always comes between the subject and the object, just as for Locke the primary and secondary qualities did. These two sets of qualities are still there, but so are a number of others which now share that position.

The material object is as unknowable for Kant as it was for Locke. All that we can know are the properties we attribute to it, and they are many indeed! So many in fact that, as we have noted, Kant had to assume that the mind, that is to say, conscious awareness, has the ability to unify all of the elements which enter into experience. When a man sees a chair, say, his mind does the following. First off it makes it possible for him to see it extended in space and enduring in time. Second of all, it makes a selection of the categories; it has a color, a shape, a location in space and a period of time, and so on. The mind does all this, but without accomplishing very much, because, in a word, *time*, *space* and the *categories*, which are the devices by means of which we have any experiences at all, also interpose a veil between us and the world, so that we cannot ever know the chair as it really is.

Kant's was a brave attempt to analyze experience, using all of the previous information available to him. The only trouble with it is that it has many fatal flaws. For instance, given the pair, *appearance-and-reality*, Kant made of his act of experience merely one of appearance. Like Locke, he said that the *reality* of the material object, the chair, the *thing-as-it-is-in-itself*, is forever unknowable. In this way, he ruled out all reliable knowledge of the external world, which may or may not correspond to its appearance. If the appearance *is* the reality there would be no need to distinguish between them, but since we do distinguish, it suggests a difference. And so what Kant was saying about reliable knowledge of reality was that it cannot be had.

The overriding doubt in his system makes us suspicious of all knowledge! And the doubt finally must be extended to Kant's theory itself. For if his picture is true of how knowledge works according to experience, and if experience is to be our only touchstone, then it would be fair to ask Kant: how does he know all this? Did he in fact experience his theory of experience? I think that he would have to admit that he did not but that he assumed it. How else could he have started with it? But in that case it is not a theory based on experience but instead a theory *about* experience based on something else. Behind Kant's theory of knowledge there lies an unexamined theory of reality.

We can see now what the trouble is. Kant had a firm grasp of many of the elements that go to make up human sense experience. But when he sought to explain them, he made the mistake of putting them all together *inside the subject*. For instance take time and space. These don't sound very internal, do they? We ordinarily think of time as the way in which things last, and we think of space as where they are situated. Not so Kant. He insisted on relating them to the subject, more particularly to consciousness. Time, he said, is the internal sense and space the external sense. Everything for him had to be explained in terms of a relation to the awareness of the individual.

Kant's philosophy appeals to people as giving the view from ground level. No dubious constructions, no high-flown metaphysics. But the truth is that Kant's whole theory of knowledge is as much of a construction as, say, Plato's theory of the Ideas. Kant's theory is hung on experience, but no one ever experienced Kant's *experience* any more than he experienced Plato's *theory* of the Ideas.

Kant evidently forgot or ignored Hume's caution that action demonstrates forcefully the existence of an external world. Indeed, what our experience does tell us is that the external world is independent of us. In other words, experience discloses a world which does not depend for its existence upon our experience of it.

That should not be very hard to see. But it does torpedo Kant's whole system. No one can believe any longer that the world depends upon our knowledge of it. Kant's claim is too wide. But, like all great systems of philosophy, it did make an impact and it does leave a residue of truth.

That residue is contained in the insight that we do have a unified point of view, and that we observe the world from the perspective of our own beliefs. It is like a poker player who holds his cards very close to his belt. Each one of us has his own philosophy, based on a system of ideas that he believes in. It may be narrow but it is for the most part consistent. The only trouble, unfortunately, is that the world is a larger place than any of our limited schemes of understanding would indicate. Sooner or later something intrudes upon our attention that we had not included. Novelty and surprises keep breaking in and making a hash of our little private philosophies.

Kant tried to take account of that fact, too. One of his achievements was to see where the limits of reasoning lay. He took his readers on a tour of the frontiers of knowledge, and showed them some examples of its limitations. He found such limitations in time, space, and matter, for instance. Of time and space, it makes as much sense to say that they are completed and finite as to say that they are incomplete and infinite. We simply cannot know. The same is true of the divisibility of matter: can it be divided indefinitely or not? It makes as much sense one way as the other. He found the same things to be true of a first cause for the world and for its necessity.

His answer was that all of these ideas imply a totality of the universe, and the totality lies beyond human experience. If experience is still to be the touchstone, then here are the limits of knowledge, this is where experience comes to an end. And it ends shortly before reaching the totality of the universe. The great illusion is that we can have such knowledge of the totality.

If this is the case, then what about that greatest of all illusions, the existence of God? Surely God is not part of our limited experience. Does this mean then that He does not exist? Kant's answer is that we need Him and so we must think of Him as existing.

All of our activity is directed toward the answers to three fundamental questions, Kant said. These are: "What can I know?" "What should I do?" "What may I hope?" We have seen what his answer was to the first; now let us look at how he treated the other two.

We have come to the end of Kant's theories of knowledge and reality. But like most great philosophers he was a comprehensive thinker. He had a theory of morality also, and since it has become a famous one, I had better tell you about it here. It contains the answer to his first question, "What should I do?"

Morality is concerned primarily with the good. Now nothing, Kant flatly asserted, can be called absolutely good except the good will. Where that good will led, Kant followed; and it led him to set up a moral law. You should act as though you could will your action to become universal in nature. That, he said, *is* the moral law, and it is compulsory. He called it therefore the *Categorical Imperative.* He meant by this that it was the first necessary command of all human behavior. It led him to a more practical rule. He said that we should treat each person as though he were an end in himself and never as a means to our own ends.

Something like this had been said before, first probably by Confucius some 500 years before our era, and then by Jesus. But Kant placed it in a philosophical framework. For it we need, he thought, three beliefs. We need to believe in God, in freedom and in immortality. Here, then, is the answer to Kant's third question, what may I hope? We can hope that there is a God, that we do in fact have freedom, and that we will surely be rewarded with immortality.

Do these exist? Kant's answer was that whether they exist or not, we need them. We need them because morality would be impossible to defend without them. And so, begging the question of their existence, it is enough to say not that they must exist but only that we must believe in them.

To construct such a picture of morality Kant had to assume that you could will such beliefs as you needed, that, in short, belief is at the mercy of the will. We shall find much later that this may not be the case. I can give you an example here, however, of how it led Kant himself astray.

Like all humanists, Kant was opposed to war. His thoughts turned to the possibility of "perpetual peace," and in an essay he discussed it at some length. He acknowledged that the natural state of man was one of war (as indeed Hobbes had declared), and that consequently perpetual peace could not be achieved unless it had first been established in some way.

To establish it, there would have first to be a set of pre-conditions, followed by a set of principles upon which all the states would agree. The pre-conditions included not making treaties with secret reservations concerning a future war, not interfering with each other's independence, the abolition in time of all standing armies, etc. Then the following principles would have to be universally adopted: that the form of every state be republican, that the law of nations be founded on a federation of free states, and that the rights of man include universal hospitality.

Kant thought that this "harmony could spring from the human discord, even against the will of man." This was not evident, he thought, but was one of "the cunning contrivances of nature." The "commercial spirit" (for which read manufacture and trade) overrides every other consideration, he said, and since trade is incompatible with war, war must go. "For, of all the forces which lie at the command of a state, the power of money is probably the most reliable. Hence states find themselves compelled—not, it is true, exactly from motives of morality—to further the noble end of peace and to avert war."

For Kant the way in which the French Revolution of 1789 had promoted the republican form of government and the fact that other states remained more or less aloof gave strong support to his theory that perpetual peace was on the way. But as everyone knows now, this was not to be the case, and so Kant's optimism was not justified.

Kant may have been the first to dream of a global state in which every individual would be a citizen. It was to be reached through a Federation of Nations. Kant recognized that without an international authority having a force higher than that of the separate states there could be no international state. Our subsequent experience with the League of Nations and now with the United Nations would seem to bear him out. Even now all international arrangements and the settlement of disputes between the various states—and especially those between the strongest states—go around the United Nations rather than through it.

Although Kant's philosophy was based on experience, he saw man as pre-eminently rational, by which he meant consciously and deliberately given over to reason, and so Kant's political theory is perfectly consistent with his theory of knowledge. Unfortunately, there is much in man which he omitted to take into account, to say nothing of the fact that social life is complex and interests conflict in many forceful ways.

Human beings on the whole are far from simple, and everyone is at least two people. Kant was no exception. It is possible to find a great person who is a small thinker—that is fairly common—but it is possible also to find a great thinker who is a small person. Kant belonged to the latter type.

He was not the kind of man anyone could love, and evidently nobody tried. He defined marriage as the mutual lease of the sexual organs, ignoring all of the emotions and sentiments which play so large a part. His life was so regular that housewives could set their watches by the time when he took his walk every afternoon. It is said that he was very fond of a particular kind of imported candy, and once the supply failed because the ship bringing it had encountered a fierce storm and had lightened cargo by dumping, among other things, his candy. Kant was irked and insisted that they had not had a moral right to save their ship in this way.

Whether your philosophy calls on you to look for the reality *behind* the appearances, or whether it requires you to look for the reality *in* the appearances by connecting them, the result is a philosophy based on the theory of knowledge. In the former case Kant will serve you very well as a guide, in the latter case we must find someone else for you and, as we will next discover, this can be done. I might remind you, however, that it is not always necessary to make a division between appearance and reality in such a fundamental way. Many of the greatest of the Greek philosophers did not and there are philosophers among us today who still do not.

Just as the philosophy of Aquinas became in time the "approved" philosophy of the Roman Catholic Church, so in time the philosophy of Kant was drawn on as though he had made a theology for the Protestant religions. Kant's philosophy in a way represented the results of the impact of the appeal to common sense translated into both secular and religious terms, religion within the limits of reason and sense experience. That explains its enormous appeal in the century that followed its appearance. Philosophers today are still inclined to insist that even if you do not agree with Kant you have to answer him, you cannot ignore him or go around him. I am not so sure. Still, it is important to have read him, provided always that you do not get stuck with his viewpoint, as indeed so many have.

Thirty-four years before Kant died, another German philosopher was born who was to equal if not surpass him in influence. The name of the new philosopher was Hegel. He was not only a critic of Kant's philosophy but perhaps the man who made the most arrogant claims for the importance of his own that had ever been made by anyone. We could laugh at this a little more easily if he had not been taken so seriously.

Many philosophers would say today that Hegel, born in 1770, was one of the four greatest philosophers in the western tradition, the other three being Plato, Aristotle and Kant. I must warn my readers, however. When you read Hegel (and I don't recommend that to any but the hardiest thinkers), take a deep breath first, for you may get dizzy following his arguments when he goes round and round with his perpetual zigzagging.

Hegel was a careful student and his originality developed slowly. He was correct and conservative in his private life, and entertained a great respect for the institution of the family and even more for the state. When Napoleon defeated the Prussians at the battle of Jena, Hegel lost his professorship and was forced to support his family by editing a newspaper and serving as the headmaster of a boys' school. But he kept on writing and ten years later accepted a professorship at Heidelberg which he kept for two years before moving to the University of Berlin. He died a victim of the cholera epidemic of 1831.

Hegel was so sure he was right that he almost did not have to be condescending, only tolerant and patronizing. His system was all-enveloping, and he thought that he had explained everything, even God. For everything has its own logic and Hegel knew what that logic is.

Someone has said, only half jokingly, that to understand Hegel's philosophy you must first have understood it. There is a germ of truth in this remark. There is an all-at-onceness to it, which in fact he intended. Let me see then how well I can explain it.

Hegel took seriously the claim of the ancient Greek philosopher, Parmenides, that the whole of the universe is more real than its parts. He also took seriously Socrates' method of debate, the so-called *dialectic,* in which two men argue until together they arrive at the truth. For Hegel reality is a process, and moves with what he called its own *logic,* which is the dialectic of three separate movements: a "thesis," or beginning; an opposite, called the *antithesis;* and a resolution of the two in a third, called the *synthesis.* The process does not stop there, for the *synthesis* of the one movement is the *thesis* of the next.

Hegel's reasoning was not linear, not all in a line the way the reasoning of previous philosophers had been. It was circular and concerned only wholes and parts. All things, not merely all organisms, are more than the sums of their parts. The truth, the reality and the value of anything depends in this way upon everything else. Everything—every part and every whole—must count for its reality upon the whole.

This then is Hegel's conception of the nature of reality. He said that it is an Absolute but then he conceived the absolute as a process, not a substance. The real is the rational, for him, and the rational the real.

Hegel took over all of the old classifications or *categories* which Kant had collected from his predecessors, and made them into dialectic movements in groups of three. I will give some examples.

His first division of three categories is that into *Being, Nature* and *Spirit*. Being is "Reason in itself" (in German, *an sich*); Nature is "Reason for itself" (*für sich*); and Spirit is Reason "reflected back into itself" (*an und für sich*).

At the human level we find a triad of categories of *subjective, objective* and *absolute spirits*. Hegel did not use the word "spirit" in the way in which it had been used before but in his own way. And since he did not define it, we can only guess at what he meant, guiding ourselves by what else he said. By *spirit*, then, he seems to have meant something like *conscious aim*.

He then said that there was a *subjective spirit*, which gave rise to its opposite, the *objective spirit*. You begin, he thought, with yourself, your ego. But in all of Hegel's writings there are wheels within wheels. The subject contains within itself a triad: *sensation*, which is the bare presence of experience; *perception*, upon which the attention is fixed; and *understanding*, by which universals are derived from things and regarded as their essences.

But to set the subject apart as an all-important subject of knowledge, it has to be put in opposition to the object, the other, which the subject, in a sense generates for itself. Thus for there to be a subject at all, there has to be an object. He did not say so but he was talking of course about the conscious self. The spirit of consciousness leads us to the contents of consciousness, which is the object. The object is rational, and in its turn is divided into three movements: the *theoretic spirit*, or conscious thought; the *practical spirit;* and, from their unity, the *free spirit*.

Now we have a *subjective spirit*, with its subdivision into a dialectic movement, and an *objective spirit*, similarly divided. The resolution of the two is the *absolute spirit*, which subordinates but exceeds the previous two. As we should have come to expect by now, Hegel divided the absolute spirit further into another dialectic. These three he called *art, religion* and *philosophy*. We are drawing close to the end. *Art* and *religion* are opposites, and they are resolved by *philosophy*, which is the highest of all human enterprises. By *philosophy*, he meant of course, his own philosophy, which was higher still, the highest of all.

However, let me list some of the other movements of the dialectic as Hegel saw them: *being* and *non-being*, resolved by *becoming; essence* and *existence*, resolved by *change; actuality* and *potentiality*, resolved by *fact;* and so on.

By these movements Hegel did not mean to describe a process which takes place in time and passes on. He meant rather a permanent set of relationships which are arranged in a sort of time-order but are not happening in time.

Sometimes, however, he did seem to ignore this difference himself, and confused temporal succession with logical order. For instance, it was Hegel who established the three historical divisions in the history of western philosophy: the Greek, the medieval and the modern, as we teach it still today.

It was Hegel, too, who saw all of history in terms of the same dialectical structure. First there was Asia, he said, with its lack of individual freedom, its childishness and its social chaos. Asia gave way to the partial freedom and order of Greece and Rome, with its conscious individuality and its lack of infinite aspirations. The final synthesis of the two was Europe. European culture had its own supreme dialectic in the Reformation, the Renaissance and then the German Enlightenment.

No one has been more penetrating in his vision of human affairs, and no one more foolish, than Hegel was occasionally. Let me give you an example of each to show what I mean.

On the penetrating side was his understanding of the relation of the great man to his times, the culture-hero who reflects and is reflected by the events of his day. If this observation seems obvious now, it is because Hegel made it so.

On the foolish side was Hegel's view of China as "infantile."

The evidence he offered us was that the Chinese language sounded like baby-talk! To him, of course, not to a Chinese.

He wrote well, and often with humor. Of Schelling's unrelieved idealism, he said that it sounded "like a night in which all cows were black." He is famous for having observed that "no man is a hero to his valet," but it is usually forgotten that he added, "not because the hero is no hero, but because the valet really is a valet."

Hegel's dialectical philosophy was suggested to him by other philosophers, particularly by Fichte and Schelling, but his political theory was the result of his recognition that Germany, unlike most western nations, was not a state but only a loose collection of independent principalities which lacked even the power to defend itself. In this it resembled Italy but differed from France, England and Spain. Hegel recognized that Germany was a nation culturally but one which had never learned how to subordinate its various parts to a whole.

The Germans were slaves, he insisted, because anarchy is not freedom. True freedom is to be found only within the bounds of a nation state. He recognized that Germany would never become unified by depending upon the consent of the people. He did not shrink from the consequences: it is in war, he said, not peace, that a nation achieves its greatest potentiality.

The state is not limited to the same morality as its private citizens, for the state knows no higher duty than to preserve and strengthen itself. It is the interdependence of the institutions, economic, moral and legal, which makes the state morally superior to civil society. This view enabled Hegel to discard the rights of man, those liberties of the individual which the French and British had made so much of. Instead, he thought the citizen could find his highest freedom in the service of the state.

In Germany the state had meant too little, and Hegel was determined to correct that deficiency, but in so doing he bent over too far on the other side and made it mean too much. He declared it to be nothing less than the spiritual embodiment of a people's will and destiny, "the real realm of freedom in which the Idea of Reason has to materialize itself." The state became, in a word, the progressive realization of the *World-Spirit.*

Hegel never lived to see his dream of a unified Germany come true. He died in 1831, still thinking it would happen under Austrian leadership. Thirty-six years later the North German Confederation was assembled and adopted a constitution, with a centralized military system, under the command of the King of Prussia, with Bismarck as Chancellor. In 1870 Germany fought and won a war against France.

Hegel had a very good opinion of the worth of what he had accomplished. He thought that his philosophy—and by inference himself—was the highest point history had ever reached. He would never have said what Joe E. Lewis, the night club comedian, once said to an enthusiastic audience: "Just think of me as an ordinary god."

Hegel may be the most comprehensive expression of what one scholar, E. M. Butler, has called "the tyranny of Greece over Germany." Her thesis is that because the rediscovery of Greek culture came to Germany last of all the west European countries, it hit very hard. The Germans thought of themselves as the latter-day Athenians with an arrogance which has rarely been matched in modern times.

You can tell how large a thinker's influence is when you see that he has followers in two extremely opposite camps, both of whom claim him. Hegel was admired by the British idealists, who scorned action in favor of thought, and by the German revolutionists, who scorned thought in favor of action! Both owed much to Hegel's philosophy.

The man who was known to have hated Hegel most was the next thinker we have to consider, his contemporary, Arthur Schopenhauer (1788-1860). Hegel was given one of the most important academic posts, he was the leading professor of philosophy at the prestigious University of Berlin, a post which Schopenhauer thought he himself should have had.

Some philosophers are perfect reflections of the times in which their authors lived, others are more the expressions of personalities. Schopenhauer's philosophy was influenced by his predecessors but was chiefly the result of his own peculiarities. His father was a wealthy banker who provided for him for life. When he was given the opportunity to lecture at the University of Berlin he scheduled his lectures at the same time as the very popular Hegel, and so no students attended. He withdrew in anger, and spent the remainder of his life writing philosophy.

He never married, conducted a number of affairs himself but resented his mother's life after his father died. She was a writer of popular novels and essays and kept a salon where she attracted younger men. He quarreled with her and stopped seeing her during the last twenty-four years of her life. The result was that he hated women. He was ill-mannered, irritable and egotistical. When fame finally came to him toward the end, it was almost too late.

Schopenhauer had two great philosophical truths to give to the world. The first of these was his theory of the will, the second was his theory of art.

The first of these was contained in his theory of reality. Reality for him was the *will*, but what he meant by the *will* was not merely a conscious and active response in the human individual.

The *will* for Schopenhauer was not just a psychological impulse. That was what the word had always meant, and it meant that for Schopenhauer, too. But that was not all it meant. It meant a world-force, something like what we now call in physics *energy;* and it was that part of the world-force which resides in the individual that has been called the will. For the human will is energy, too, human energy.

The will as Schopenhauer saw it is blind, ungovernable and destructive. Schopenhauer's *will* is best compared to Kant's *self* and his *material object*, which were unknowable in themselves. The will, Schopenhauer thought, was a *thing-in-itself*, above time and space, and uncaused. Because of the work of the will, always seeking to preserve itself against all others, he saw existence itself as consisting in conflict, suffering and indeed evil.

Was there no escape from such a destructive force? Schopenhauer saw three ways to deal with it. The first two were, literally, escapes. You could escape into the intellectual world of the Platonic Ideas by means of a life of contemplation. Or you could escape into the sublime world of the fine arts.

In the third way, you turn to face your will, directing it against itself. Since the will is essentially a will to live, you have to deny it. Turn the will against itself and will not to will. Admittedly, this would leave life with very little. Hegel accepted the consequences of this argument. It is best, he thought, to withdraw from the world and from all worldly things and to become an ascetic.

This third way recommended by Schopenhauer came out somewhere near what Buddha had recommended some 500 years B.C. Life, Buddha said, contains little but pain and suffering, which are the products of desire. Once you have a desire, you will end with pain, for either the desire will be satisfied and that will lead to the pain of satiation, or the desire will be unsatisfied, and unsatisfied desire is always painful. Get rid, then, of all desire, including the desire to live, and you will get rid of pain.

The effort by which you deny your own will to live, Schopenhauer concluded, comes from something in you deeper than the will itself, something supernatural and of a divine grace that arrives from outside. It feels like a positive bliss, beyond all thought and all speech, and so is very much worth the striving for.

I have said above that Schopenhauer brought us two great philosophical truths. The first of these was the destructive nature of the will. The second was his theory of art. It is in fact the theory of art that Plato should have written instead of the one that he did, because it is more consistent with Plato's metaphysics than with Schopenhauer's.

In experiencing works of art, we have the sense that we are triumphing over the hostile aspects of the commonplace. By contemplating through objects which are friendly the beauty which we see in them, we rise above the terror of the will, to the level of those Ideas of which Plato told us. It is in the world of Platonic Ideas that we find our greatest comfort.

Schopenhauer was perhaps the first philosopher who did not look at the world and see it as what he would like it to be. So many philosophers have mistaken what-is for what-ought-to-be that it might well be called "the philosopher's error."

It is a very long distance from things-as-they-are to things-as-they-ought-to-be, so far, in fact, that it is seldom travelled. Philosophers ought to recognize that they have not done enough when they have set up an ideal. They must tell us also how to get to it from where we are.

Schopenhauer was the first philosopher in a long line to give due credit to the ugly side of life. Most philosophers have painted only the rosy side because of course it was the side they preferred. Kant even went so far as to declare that "man is the final purpose of the whole of nature." Admittedly, life has two sides, but if we neglect the ugly one, we will never design the proper strategy for getting from it to the one we prefer.

I am sorry to have to tell you that Schopenhauer's philosophy of art did not have the influence it should have had. What did have an influence was the new moral theory of the Englishman Jeremy Bentham (1748-1832). Like Schopenhauer, Bentham inherited wealth but, unlike Schopenhauer, he was possessed of a benign spirit. Life had been made easy for him and as a consequence everything seemed simple.

Bentham rejected as "fiction" the social contract and sought something more basic as a foundation for social action. He found it in the "fact" of Utility. He called his new moral theory *utilitarianism*, a word which has been much used ever since. By it he meant that the highest moral good is "the greatest happiness of the greatest number" of people. An action is useful if it contributes to this condition, and is not if it does not.

Good and evil themselves, he said, were based on pleasure and pain. Every act must be considered together with its consequences, and these can be measured by the intensity and duration of the pleasure it produces minus the pain by which it is attended. Bentham thought in fact that a calculus of pleasure and pain could be worked out. We pursue pleasure and so the good, and avoid pain and with it evil. All social institutions, including the economic ones and especially the state, should be guided accordingly.

One of his followers, John Stuart Mill (1806-1873), pointed out, however, that some pleasures were higher than others, the intellectual for instance higher than the sensual. Moreover, Mill said that man is naturally altruistic: individual happiness of the highest sort lies in promoting the happiness of others.

Mill is almost the only case on record of a planned personality, a man designed to be an original thinker who actually became one. An extraordinary story. Mill's father, on the advice of Bentham, saw to it that his son learned Greek at the age of three. By four he was teaching it to his sister. He also learned arithmetic and English grammar almost as soon, and by the age of eight he was deep in Latin. Religion played little part in his education and he had no time for games or sport. He wrote philosophy all of his life but made a living working for the East India Company. In his middle age he fell in love with a married woman and married her two years after her husband's death. He discussed all of his work with her and gave her credit for much of it. She died at Avignon when they were on a trip, and was buried there. So great was his devotion that he remained at Avignon the last fifteen years of his life in order to be near her grave.

He is known chiefly for his analysis of the logic of experimental inquiry. In the search for order among masses of facts, his analysis is unsurpassed. Mill thought that there were "real kinds" of things in nature, which accounted for the uniformity which can be found there. He distinguished a number of ways in which phenomena vary together and these have taken their place as a valid part of the scientific method.

Influences which come to philosophy from science are not compacted all of a piece. They come occasionally, and one at a time. Most powerful of all that occurred in the middle of the nineteenth century was the theory of biological evolution published by Charles Darwin. Life consists, he announced, in a struggle for existence; the strongest species were the fittest to survive, and so they won out over the others.

The part of his theory that had the greatest impact, however, concerned the descent of man. Darwin's discovery was that man and monkey had a common ancestry: that the early apes were the ancestors of both, and that intermediate types could be found. The theory is secure now that a wealth of evidence had been uncovered, but at the time it roused a storm of controversy because it challenged the account of man's origin in Genesis. The religious leaders were profoundly disturbed and grew almost hysterical at the suggestion that man was a risen ape rather than a fallen angel.

The influence of Darwin's theory spread far beyond the ancient history of man's origins. The evolution of organic species became a commonplace in zoology, but there was much more. The history of everything became a standard part of its explanation. How things came to be what they are could be used now to account in part at least for what they are.

The history of an important new discovery is usually the history also of the wrong interpretations of it. In fact, fame may be said to consist in a sufficient number of misunderstandings. In Darwin's case I will report two errors which, alas, have been influential.

The theory of the evolution of the species has been used as an argument against Plato's theory of the Ideas. Since Aristotle first introduced the names, both *genus* and *species* have been understood to be fixed and eternal universals, that is to say, Platonic Ideas. But if they can change and evolve, they are neither fixed nor eternal, the argument runs. The argument rests, however, on the false notion that there are only a limited and finite number of species. There is no reason to suppose that. Between one species and another which evolved from it there could be any number of species, each a universal or Platonic Idea. Evolution is the process in which an animal moves from one species to another, and such a move can be repeated any number of times, as many times in fact as there are adjacent species.

To explain the second error it will be necessary to introduce another philosopher. His name was Herbert Spencer (1820-1903) and for a while he became the most famous thinker of the nineteenth century. He was consulted by kings and emperors. He had begun life as a practicing engineer, but changed to writing after he read Darwin's *Origin of Species* (1859). We would say now that he over-reacted, because he projected and finished a vast system of philosophy in many volumes based on the single idea of organic evolution. As strong as that idea was it was not enough to carry such a project all by itself.

Spencer was so struck by Darwin's theory of evolution that he used it to explain everything. Only, he made a serious mistake. He thought that Darwin had meant that the strongest *individuals* were best fitted to survive and could thereby justify the use of force in overcoming their fellows. This theory, which has come to be called "social Darwinism" has had a disastrous effect. Because it seemed to justify strong-arm methods of winning the struggle for existence, it has been used by ruthless seekers after power, for instance by those modern bully-boys, the fascists.

What Darwin had meant of course was nothing like this. He had meant that the *species* which was best fitted to survive did so, the strongest *species*, not the strongest *individuals*. They are by no means the same.

The effect of Darwin's discovery, however, has not been confined to biology. Ever since, anything in need of explanation has been explained partly at least by showing how it got to be what it is. Darwin was responsible for the theory of development that has run right through all of the sciences. Physics calls its theory of the origin and development of the universe *cosmology* and chemistry seeks the origin of the chemical elements. Social studies look to the development of social institutions, and anthropology is interested in the study of primitive cultures on the theory that they have something to tell us about the development of present day society.

The history of philosophy is for the most part an account of the smooth workings of things, of the setting forth of ideals. But in the nineteenth century a change occurred. Quite suddenly it was understood that all was not well in human affairs and that the philosophers had not taken sufficient account of the destructive side of man's nature. It is difficult to talk about ideals in all seriousness when there are so many conflicts in society. Some philosophers at the time, I might add, did not elect to take the subjective by-pass but instead ploughed straight ahead into the thick of events.

The first thinker to give conflict its due was Schopenhauer, the second was Nietzsche, and the third was Marx. I have already discussed Schopenhauer's ideas; the next great figure in European philosophy we shall have to examine therefore is Nietzsche.

Friedrich Nietzsche was born in 1844 to a German family which had produced many Lutheran pastors, but he elected to become a philologist specializing in Greek and Latin literatures, and won several scholarships. His father died when he was four, and he was raised by women; his mother, two maiden aunts and an adoring sister. While still relatively young he was appointed to a professorship at the University of Basel. He left it to do his military service in the Horse Artillery. In training, while mounting a horse, he was thrown against the pommel and injured his chest. At the end of a year of illness he returned to civilian life.

He had a famous friendship with the composer Richard Wagner whom he admired greatly, but he broke with him over Wagner's anti-Semitism. Nietzsche's sister unfortunately seems to have sympathized with Wagner. Nietzsche had for some time made plans to pursue a life of scholarship, and when the Franco-Prussian War began in 1870 Nietzsche, who had meantime become a Swiss citizen, found he could not engage in combat and so entered the ambulance service where he worked long and hard hours and made himself ill again. He therefore returned to his professorship but his poor health would not allow him to continue, and he retired to a private life devoted to writing. In 1889 he suffered a stroke after which he never fully recovered his sanity. In his last years he was cared for by his mother and sister.

Students profess to find in his later work signs of madness, but no one doubts its brilliance. Apart from its contents it is known for a literary style which has attracted many readers, including those who were not primarily interested in his philosophy.

This has happened to few philosophers. Before Nietzsche, among the philosophers whose work appealed to those interested in literature the names of Plato and Schopenhauer occur first. After Nietzsche, the names which come to mind in this connection are those of the French philosopher Henri Bergson and the American George Santayana.

Nietzsche stands outside the scientific tradition altogether because he was the first great philosopher of culture. He was not concerned with any one institution but rather with the comparison of whole human cultures. When he talked about the individual it was always in this connection.

He was critical of Darwin for insisting that all species should submit to influences from the environment, when, according to Nietzsche, it was the painful duty of the human species to struggle against the environment. He was critical of Schopenhauer for the same sort of reason. Schopenhauer's philosophy meant for the individual that he should assume a negative and a passive attitude, based on weakness, but Nietzsche thought that it was the happy duty of the individual to be strong and aggressive. Nietzsche insisted that the strong man loves power and affirms the will to live.

Nietzsche's social message was that we should give up Christianity and return to the pagan virtues of Greek civilization. The Greeks worshipped the value of sweet reasonableness which they expressed in the arts in the shape of a God of calmness and serenity, Apollo. They worshipped also the values of ecstasy and intoxication, of the passionate intensity of enjoyment and of orgies, represented by the God Dionysus. Nietzsche thought that the Greeks had known how to mix these forces into a proper blend which carried them to the heights of civilization. The cause of the sudden and tragic decline of Greece came from the dissociation and consequent opposition of the Apolline and the Dionysiac.

Christianity, however, came to supplant the Greek values with its own, bringing weakness with it and a "nay-saying." Socrates had begun the decline by insisting on a passive intellectual life in place of an active one. Christianity with its moral demands continued the decline, until all the power had been drained from existence.

What was needed, then, to restore western civilization to its full and former state of vigor was to bring back the old Greek values, reaffirm the "Will to Power," and once more fuse the Apolline with the Dionysiac. Man then would be restored in his dignity and grandeur to the essential tragedy of existence. Nietzsche believed that civilization in his day was at the bottom of the curve and he could only swing upward from there, beginning with the rebirth of the influence of Dionysus.

That was Nietzsche's social message. His message to the individual was along the same lines. He cast these reflections in literary form, in a work of fiction which purported to be the testament of a Persian prophet, Zoroaster. Using a slightly archaic spelling he composed a book, translated into English as *Thus Spoke Zarathustra*. In it he continued his affirmations of the will to power by calling on that will to surpass itself.

It would do this he thought by producing the Superman. Nietzsche's Superman is not the superman of the comic strips in the Sunday supplements of our newspapers. He was a man who could exercise great physical strength and courage to overcome his opposition, but what made him so superior was his greatness of soul and his firmness of character. Christian ethics had been a "slave-morality." What Nietzsche advocated in his conception of the Superman was a "master-morality."

Curiously, while Nietzsche had rejected Christianity, he did not reject Christ. Christianity was the work of Paul. True *Christ*-ianity had never been tried because, as he said, "the last Christian died on the Cross."

There would be in the future a "Twilight of the [old] Gods" and a "transmutation of all values," with Dionysus and Christ arising together to dramatize their triumph over death and their new affirmation of the will to power for all men who are strong. Led by the Superman among them, they would go beyond fear and pity and indeed beyond all good and evil to a glorious affirmation of art and of existence itself.

Nietzsche has been claimed by the existentialists, whose philosophy we are presently to examine. As I hope to show, this is unjustified. On the other hand, he has been accused of having been the philosopher of the Italian fascists and the German Nazis because he seemed to be saying the same thing they were saying about the triumph of the strong. This too is unjustified. Nietzsche spoke warmly of the Jews and disparagingly of the Germans. But in principle he was opposed to the idea that any race was superior to any other, and his Superman was one who exercised moral strength rather than brute force.

Chapter XII

The Greatest
European Philosophers II

The nineteenth century was an astonishing period in philosophy, for it was then that science had its greatest successes and that philosophy twisted and turned in an effort to adjust to it. In this and the following chapter we shall see how some important and influential philosophers avoided the subjective by-pass. After that we shall see how others devoted themselves exclusively to it.

If the decision of philosophers was not to take the subjective by-pass, then they had to cope with science directly. They did so with varying results.

The philosopher who recommended a complete surrender to science was one who had the least influence outside of philosophy. He was a Frenchman and his name was Auguste Comte. He called his philosophy *positivism*. In it he suggested that history had been marked by three stages of growth. First there was the religious stage, then there was the philosophical, and finally there was the positive (or scientific). No need, he said, to go back to the earlier stages; now science could answer all the questions. Science, in other words, would replace both religion and philosophy, which were no longer needed. By "science" Comte meant of course the physical sciences: physics, chemistry

163

and biology. The social sciences, such as economics, politics, and sociology, he thought were backward affairs.

Comte was the first man to see that there is an order among the sciences, and that they could be arranged in an ascending scale from the simplest to the most complex. The order he gave was: mathematics, astronomy, physics, chemistry, biology and sociology. This is the arrangement which is studied today under the name of "the integrative levels in nature." With the exception of mathematics, which is more abstract, each is based on the study of materials whose complexity of organization increases upward.

Philosophy was to have its place in furthering science, which he saw as a fundamentally practical pursuit. He saw in science itself the prospects of a new society. There was to be a new science of social behavior, the "social science" that was so badly needed. It would consist in a kind of extreme humanism, and in his later years in fact he thought there could be a religion of humanity. Comte had a number of devoted followers who called themselves "Positivists" and who made faithful visits to his grave.

The man who thought he had solved the dilemma with which science confronted philosophy was named Karl Marx. He did so by claiming that philosophy and social science are one and the same thing. He was wrong, of course, but never has an error had such an impact. It is a well known fact that the scientific method has not worked as well in the social field as it has in the physical, and "social science" remains a hope rather than an accomplishment. Yet Marx's philosophy has been accepted by millions of people as their way of life, enough people to make his ideas equal in influence with those of the great religious leaders.

There are other reasons for the astonishing acceptance of Marx's philosophy. It had an obvious and immediate application to economic and political life. In addition the decline of Christianity was leaving a vacuum which had to be filled somehow, since men cannot live without a metaphysical belief of some sort, and the ideas of Marx were there to fill the gap. His life spans most of the nineteenth century, but the impact of his work has been felt chiefly in the twentieth century and is being felt more than ever today.

Marx was a German and a member of the "young German" party whose members were devoted to social reform. He opposed bitterly the established economic and political order of his day and never stopped attacking it. After several unsuccessful attempts to lead the German workers in a social revolution, he fled to England where he took no more part in political action but instead wrote his famous books, especially *Das Capital*. He worked largely in the British Museum library, and was supported by Friedrich Engels, another German and the son of a rich factory owner in Manchester.

The philosophy of Marx and Engels—for it was a complete philosophy, with a theory of reality as well as prescriptions for social and political action—has come to be called "Marxism" for short. Its practice has been known as "communism." It is now the official doctrine of two of the most powerful states in the modern world, the Soviet Union and mainland China. It has been adopted also in some smaller countries, for instance in Yugoslavia, Czechoslovakia, Albania and Cuba.

The influences which went to make up the theory and practice of the philosophy which Marx and Engels wrote and which has come to be called *dialectical materialism* were many. Their virtue was to see the connections among the influences and to make one grand synthesis. They were influenced by the anarchists who recommended violent revolution but wished to substitute nothing for the governments which were to be overthrown. Had not Bakunin declared that "the joy of destruction is a creative joy"? They were influenced by a German philosopher named Ludwig Feuerbach who held that only matter is real and that there is no God. They were influenced also by Hegel and took over Hegel's *dialectic*. The difference was that where the *dialectic* for Hegel was ideal and therefore mental, for Marx it was to be *materialistic*, the movement of matter. Marx said that he found Hegel standing on his head and stood him on his feet. They were influenced by the French social theorist, Sorel, who had maintained that all "property is theft." They were influenced by the French Saint-Simon, who advanced the theory of the class struggle.

Marx and Engels were interested in the economic and political relations of man, man in society, not individual man. They had the idea that economic relations determine all other relations, including the political. In terms of economic interest, society has always been divided into social classes. There is always a lowest class. Anciently it was the slaves, next above them the class of free men who had no property, and finally the property-holding classes, the landed aristocracy.

Although there were slaves in the United States, in Marx's Europe there were no slaves but there were men without property whose only way of making a living was to work with their hands. In England and Germany the factory system was just coming up and with it a new laboring class, the factory workers. Marx's name for them was the *proletariat*, an old Roman word for free men without property. He thought that their interests were opposed to those of the burghers, or *bourgeoisie* as the French called them, the inhabitants of the new towns that grew up around the factories.

The men who owned and operated the factories collected the profits. Marx thought that they collected not only their own profits but also the part of the profits which rightfully belonged to the workers because it was their work which had produced the profits in the first place. He learned from an English economist named David Ricardo to think that the "labor theory of value" is correct: that the exchange value of a product is determined by the labor expended in its production. (The philosopher Locke had said something similar years earlier.) Marx gave no credit to manufacturing design, to capital investment, to all of those items which, together with the labor of the workers, go to make up the profits of the factories' output.

If you were a materialist, as Marx and Engels were, you would have to place first in your theory of reality those who worked closest to matter, those, in other words, who worked with their hands. Marx's theory was that since the members of the working class were first in theory, they should be first in practice. Since they were the most numerous, the state should be run by and for them.

History, Marx and Engels thought (for they thought as one), is an account of the class struggle for the control of the means of economic production. We are told that there is no such thing as independent truth, as the philosophers had always declared. In its place there was only the "historically correct," that is to say, the winner; whichever way history goes is the way it ought to have gone.

In a famous "manifesto" or statement of policy, he and Engels called for a bloody revolution of the working class. "Workers of the world, unite," it declared, and added, "you have nothing to lose but your chains." Their appeal to violence to make right what they considered wrongs overturned decades of humanism which had sought to eliminate violence and replace it with reason. They had before them the spectacle of the French Revolution, which had widely proclaimed the rights of man but had succeeded only in putting another class in power, which got rid of the monarchy and landed aristocracy by violent means, without achieving the ends it had sought. But the Marxists evidently learned nothing from it except the violence.

It was a fair society that they wanted to establish, one in which each individual would contribute to it what he could, and would take from it only what he needed. But there was much that was missing from the blue-prints for a better society. Marx was so concerned with the means that he forgot to fill out the details of the ends. Too bad, actually, because the men of theory, like himself and his friend Engels, were succeeded by men of practice who sought to put his ideas to work. Marx made a mistake. He thought that the revolution he was recommending would occur at the same time in all industrial countries, because economic classes are more important than nations or states. That was why his call went out to "workers of the world."

The revolution occurred instead in the most economically backward of countries, Russia. The men who made the revolution there were led by Nicolai Lenin. Lenin was a unique combination of thinker and man of action. He wrote books to show how Marx's theory should be applied, and then he applied it himself in the Russian Revolution of 1917.

Communism as a working government owes much to Lenin for both its theory and its practice. The movement has been known since his day as following the philosophy of Marx, Engels *and* Lenin. Lenin was a convinced Marxist and contributed a lot to its practice. He was responsible for the Party, understood as a working class elite distinct from the workers. He insisted on absolute and inflexible obedience to it. And it was the Party that consolidated the political and economic gains effected by the Revolution.

When Lenin died in 1924 there was a power struggle between his two chief lieutenants, Josef Stalin and Leon Trotsky. Stalin won and Trotsky fled to Mexico, where he was later murdered by Stalin's agents.

The quarrel between Stalin and Trotsky was not only a personal struggle for power but also one involving a practical question of strategy. Stalin wanted communism secured first in a single country, Russia, so that it could not be overthrown and could be used as a base for revolutionaries who were to fan out over the world from there. Trotsky's ideas were more like those of Marx and Engels, who had called for a world revolution, one which would be made in every country at the same time.

Stalin won and the result was to give communism a new turn. It became united with a nationalism as fierce as anything the old imperialists had ever contemplated. Indeed the foreign policy of Russian leaders does not seem to be any different whether those leaders are the Imperial Czars' officials or members of the Presidium of the Supreme Soviet.

We have come to see that theory is one thing and practice another. Marx had claimed that the state is an instrument of oppression in the hands of the ruling class, but if so it does not become less true when that ruling class is the communist bureaucracy. The Marxist theory as it has been applied in the Soviet Union by communists, led by Stalin and his successors, and in China by Mao-Tse-tung and his associates, bears more resemblance to the absolute dictatorship of the Czars in Russia and to the rule of the war-lords in China than it does to any ideals of socialism. A political theory which was designed to dissolve oppression and nationalism has been used instead to intensify these forces.

None of the privileges of the individual that the democracies had introduced were retained in the Soviet Union and Communist China. Individual rights, individual freedoms, individual liberties, so much cherished and protected by law in the western democracies, have not existed in communist bloc countries. Granted that the communists were dealing with larger populations than were the democracies, still the differences are painfully obvious.

What is not so obvious to observers is that the communists have raised the economic standard of living for the masses. It is not nearly so high as it is in western industrial democracies. But remember that before the revolution the Russians were serfs, illiterate and without any of the benefits of civilization. The communists have done much to improve their lot. Now they receive education, medical attention, and some at least of the consumer goods of which the people in the western countries are so enamoured. All that the masses have to do is look back to the conditions that prevailed before the revolution, and that would be sufficient incentive to get them to defend the present government with all of the power at their command.

Marx, following Hegel's dialectic, had said that the "dictatorship of the capitalist class" had to be followed by a period in which there would be a "dictatorship of the proletariat," of the working class, but that this would then be followed by a classless society. When that day came, the state would "wither away" because it would no longer be needed.

Lenin, it is well known, took a more serious view of the ultimate goal of the "withering away of the state" before he gained power than he did after. The phrase remained an embarrassment to the regime, until under Khrushchev it was revived. According to this theory, functions normally performed by the State would be taken over by public and private social organizations. But there is no evidence of this yet and nobody expects it soon.

We are presumably in the period now of the dictatorship of the proletariat, or at least so goes good Marxist theory. But neither Marx nor anyone else has ever said how long that period will last. Sometimes it takes a different sort of philosophy to operate a society than it does to start one. In the meanwhile, what we are seeing is not the dictatorship of the proletariat—of the more than two hundred and thirty million people in the Soviet Union. It is rather the dictatorship of the Communist Party. There are roughly only one million members of that Party, and membership is strictly limited. This makes of it a new privileged class. At the head of it are the dozen or two members of the Presidium of the Supreme Soviet, the rulers of all Russia.

As I write, the prediction made by Marx, that when communism had triumphed wars would be abolished, seems to have failed. Wars, he declared, are the instruments of the capitalist class to gain booty for themselves. Europe had just experienced the bloody wars of 1830 and 1848, and Marx was to see another one in 1870.

But recent events have shown that war is by no means a monopoly of the capitalists. The Soviet Union invaded Hungary with tanks in 1956, and Czechoslovakia in 1968. Both were communist countries but not deemed sufficiently subservient to the Russians. As late as 1972, the Russians were still maintaining two armored divisions in Czechoslovakia.

The competition between the Soviet Union and Communist China is intense, and a war between them could break out at any moment. The evidence seems to be, alas, that wars are human and are not confined to the rule of any nation, class, or individual.

The English historian Arnold Toynbee has somewhere called communism "the holy atheistic Church militant." The communists have always proclaimed themselves atheists, not because they could prove that God does not exist—that seems as hard to prove as that He does—but because of Marx's observation that the Church is an instrument of oppression in the hands of the ruling class and serves as "the opium of the masses."

Despite Marx's criticism of the utopian socialists, he too thought that the course of history and human progress go hand in hand. So far, the accomplishments of the communists in Asia do not seem likely to outpace those of the industrialists and democrats in Europe and America. Marx thought that capitalism would die of its own contradictions, and if it had remained as uncompromising as it seemed to him, and indeed as it was in his day, he might have been right.

Some of Marx's criticisms of capitalism were well taken. He saw that under capitalism industrial production is conducted in an orderly fashion but that there is an anarchy of exchange and distribution. He was right in thinking that social historians have neglected badly the role of economics in human life. He was wrong, however, when he supposed that a state born in conflict, exploitation and violence, which have been not only approved but encouraged, can ever take its place as a peaceful arrangement. Above all, he failed to see that his philosophy would be used to justify a dictatorship as complete and as ruthless as had ever existed.

Marx failed also to estimate the strength of capitalism under democracy. It has not died but to the contrary it has obtained new strength from its modifications. The middle class with the individual freedoms it sponsors has been able to produce the highest standard of living and the lowest death rate ever attained in civilized society.

Above all perhaps, Marx failed to predict the rise of the labor unions and of the price in high and even confiscatory taxes that the capitalists have had to pay to stay in business. The condition of the working man is very far from what it had been in Marx's day and is improving steadily. At the present time (1973), the American farmer is producing enough wheat to feed the Russians, and to help the Canadians to do the same for Communist China.

The lesson of history seems to be that the effect of a social revolution means for the masses only the exchange of one set of masters for another. When Tolstoy wrote that the rich will do anything for the poor except get off their backs, he might have said the same thing for the powerful. Jules Michelet, who discovered Vico's ideas in 1824, held that the common people are more important than their leaders, but there are few if any leaders who have ever acted as if they believed it.

Sometimes a social revolution results in a gain, sometimes in a loss, but more often in a mixture of the two. The Christian Revolution which came toward the end of the Roman Empire was responsible for a deterioration in social conditions, judged by the deplorable state of affairs which followed in the Middle Ages. On the other hand, the French Revolution of 1789 led eventually to a sharp rise in the standard of living of the middle classes made possible by capitalism, a standard which has since been extended to include the working class in all western industrial countries. The Russian Revolution of 1917 led to a considerable improvement in the living conditions of the masses in the Soviet Union but also to the rigid dictatorship of the Communist Party oligarchy.

We seem to have strayed a long way from the history of philosophy. But have we? I have spent some time on Marxism not only because it has a metaphysics but also because it shows how powerful the effects of a philosophy are when applied to the operation and direction of human affairs. Individual lives are often conducted on the basis of probabilities but societies more often rely upon absolutes. That has been true, certainly, in Medieval Europe and in the contemporary communist countries. There is nothing more dangerous than the official adoption of a metaphysics. To defend it men will not hesitate to kill.

Communism is the first example in all of history of the deliberate application of a system of philosophy to a human society. The founding of the Soviet Union was the first occasion when a philosophy was adopted by a state. There have been instances in history when a philosophy was used to defend a form of government, as with the theology of the Roman Catholic Church in the Middle Ages, for example, but never before has it been used to install one.

What John Locke's philosophy had done to defend the right to private property became, after the invention of industrial technology and heavy industry, a drawback to the well-being of the community. Too much power in too few hands led to a monopoly which could easily be used against the common good. The gigantic upheaval of communism was Marx's answer to Locke. Designed to limit private property to what the individual needs might be and so to get rid of the large measure of controls, it ended by turning over to the state the power which had proved too much for the individual. Oddly, it happened in the least developed countries and proved an instrument which was to bring them by a rapid development of economics quickly into the twentieth century to the stage which had already been reached in the western scientific-industrial countries.

But the application of Marx's ideas went too far and succeeded also in depriving the individual not only of his control of the means of production but also of his civil liberties. The communist countries in the end will have to restore those liberties, just as the democracies are having slowly to evolve a system of limited ownership. In this way the two groups of states draw closer together, though the process may require another half century to complete.

Meanwhile the outlook from where we are now is bleak though filled with wonderful opportunities. It remains to be seen which will win out, widespread war and destruction with atomic weapons, or global peace and the marvellous benefits of industrial construction.

Western civilization has for some time been inherently secular. In place of religion, it has the belief in science, which is actually a belief in the findings of reason and fact. Meanwhile the philosophers are as free as they were in ancient Greece to explore interpretations of the world which could satisfy the craving of the individual for some personal philosophy, some insights into his own perspective. It was only the most backward countries which embraced Marxism. The advanced countries which together make up western civilization, France, England, Germany, Italy, the United States, had no need of it.

I have devoted considerable space to Marx and Engels because theirs is the official philosophy in so large a part of the world now. In the western world for the most part, however, philosophy is still free, which is to say, there is no official philosophy. Perhaps it would be useful for us to remember that the Soviet Union (Chukotka Peninsula) and the United States (Alaska) are only fifty-six miles apart. Yet thus far they do not interfere with each other.

Backward from that boundary and toward the high culture centers, the characteristics intensify and the differences become sharply marked. The western world is still able to provide a large measure of individual freedom which is so essential to social development. On our side there are no limits to speculation. In such an atmosphere all sorts of philosophies have been able to gain a hearing though not many have come to prominence.

An earlier one which certainly did was the philosophy of the Frenchman Henri Bergson. He was one of the only two philosophers ever to receive a Nobel Prize for literature (the other was Bertrand Russell). Bergson belonged to that group whose philosophy has been read for its style. Like that of Russell, the influence of Bergson extended outside his profession, and, since his work was amply recognized in his profession also, that is a sign of some power.

Bergson began his philosophy by arguing against the use of reason. It distorts reality, he insisted, and handles things only from without. Intuition alone—the feelings—more akin to instinct than to intelligence, can give us the richness and vitality of experience, because intuition works from within. Bergson supposed a vital impulse not unlike Schopenhauer's "will," which is the essence of effort, and works to overcome the resistance furnished by matter.

This vital force—Bergson's name for it was *élan vital*—gives rise to matter in the very act of seeking to overcome it. But matter is everything that is dead, inert, mechanical and static, while the vital force is life itself, and life is opposed to matter, Bergson insisted. Since life is transient and matter more persistent, change is more real than permanence, he said. It is duration in time which gives things their reality. The vital impulse is what connects the generations and what is perpetuated by organic evolution.

Bergson saw a dualism in religion which is responsible for the alternation in its fortunes. On the one hand there is the conservative force of the church as an institution, and on the other hand the evolutionary force of the individual insights of men who claim a greater intuitive experience than is the lot of the ordinary individual, the saints and prophets in whose names the religions have been founded. The distinction was not a new one even in Bergson's day, but he gave it a new structure when he considered the social institution and the individual insight to be the two sources of both morality and religion.

Bergson's philosophy was weakened by his distrust of reason in favor of intuition. The one of course does not rule out the other, since reason has to have a starting-point. But the flaw lay chiefly in the fact that Bergson reasoned so strongly—against reason! If reason is unreliable, then Bergson's reasons for believing so are unreliable, too.

The nineteenth century was largely dominated by ideas of optimism and progress. In the first half of that century improvement in the human condition was regarded as almost inevitable. Everybody in Europe thought that things were getting steadily better, and the French had long been particularly inclined toward that view. Already in 1770 Sebastien Mercier had described the glories of life to come in the next seven hundred years and, as late as 1850, M.A. Javary's *The Idea of Progress* advanced the thought that progress "was the general law of history and the future of humanity."

Thanks chiefly to Darwin and the philosophers who were influenced by the idea of evolution, it was widely believed that every year conditions improved and human nature got better and better. One of the biggest publishing successes of 1908 in Europe and America was a book by Norman Angell called *The Great Illusion* in which he argued that because people had grown so civilized and had cultivated the humanistic values so whole-heartedly, never again would they resort to war for the settlement of their disputes. That was six years before the outbreak of one of the worst wars in all of history, the first world war. It shook up western civilization considerably and in fact saw the rise of international communism. The certainty of progress fell with a crash.

The philosophers perhaps did not take the war sufficiently into account. Ever since the Greeks, with few exceptions they had tried to stand aloof from the kind of social events of which they could not approve, forgetting that in any genuine attempt to understand human nature in the round, the side of it which produced so many ruthless and savage conflicts could not be neglected. The literature of war is a large one, and the novelists, poets and dramatists have seen in war the kind of experience which had an intensity they needed to record.

But there is something to be said for philosophical detachment. Like the pure sciences, philosophy can defend its right to make a contribution independently of current events, for only in that way can the timeless truths and values be discovered and their discovery announced and explained. I want to mention briefly two philosophers who, like Bergson, lived through World War I, and whose work for one reason or another has been very much neglected. Both were German.

Alexius Meinong and Nicolai Hartmann were realists, that is to say, both were interested in studying the objectivity of truths and values. Meinong was more concerned with approaching the topic through the theory of knowledge. For him there are two sets of objects which we can know but which are independent of our knowledge of them: physical or material objects, which, he said, *exist*, and logical objects or essences, which *subsist*. This is close to the two-story world of Plato, only with the reality of material objects brought up to the level of the reality of the others. The approach, unlike Plato's, was made through the process of knowing, and therefore sounds much more empirical and modern. Meinong could not quite see the objectivity of values, however. He obtained this status for them only by considering them attached to statements. His was not a full philosophy but only an epistemology.

Nicolai Hartmann's work was more comprehensive. He had not only a very well developed theory of values, in which he saw them arranged by levels in a hierarchy, but also a complete system of philosophy which belongs in the great tradition.

For Hartmann values are absolute and they are *a priori*. That is to say, material things are valuable because they have value, but the values exist not only before our knowledge of them but before the things which have value. Values in fact are eternal essences, a position which also bears comparison with what Plato asserted, though Plato's assertions were not made in the same way. Both Meinong and Hartmann were realists of the Greek variety; they tried to do what Aristotle did by grounding their theories in the objects disclosed to experience, and so appealed more to experience than Plato would have done. But they wanted to do it in order to justify the belief in the reality of the Platonic Ideas, for that is what Meinong's "subsistent objects" and Hartmann's "*a priori* values" amount to.

German realists were and still are without much influence. It was left to the British and Americans to develop a realism of their own. While their realism is not fashionable, either, it has had more influence than the German variety and is still very much with us, as we shall see in a later chapter.

Chapter XIII

Knowledge from Action Alone

Some critics of philosophy have proclaimed that it makes no progress. I do not think this is true, though I do admit that you have to look back a long way to see it. The philosophers have undertaken a big job, and they will need a long time to finish it.

There is, however, one trouble, and it is the same one the scientists often encounter. Whenever an advance is made and a problem solved, a new area of ignorance is opened up at the same time. New facts and new theories to explain them keep turning up in other fields. This means perhaps that there can be progress in the accumulation of knowledge but without ever completing it.

I will admit that the philosophers of today tend either to want to forget the classic figures of the past, on the plea that we ourselves have found the absolute truth and so there is no need to remember them; or to feel that as honest historians they must bring with them every bit of the work that has been done, dragging all of it along in their baggage, including the errors that have been defended as well as the truths that have been discovered. But this makes for an overloaded ship and there is no reason why we should lose the truth when the vessel sinks because of a cargo which consists chiefly of foolishness and of wild guesses that have long ago been disproved. I can see justification, for instance, for saving Hegel's dialectic but not for remembering his philosophy of nature or his opinion of the Chinese language.

Progress in philosophy does get interrupted at times. Other activities are going on in human life which often obscure philosophical inquiry and cause us to forget some of the best ideas of the greatest thinkers. But progress does catch up. Let me give a large example.

You will recall that in two earlier chapters we looked at the studies of men who thought that reliable knowledge could be obtained by the method of reasoning alone (Chapter VII) or by that of sense experience alone (Chapter VIII). If man has three capacities, which are for thought, for feeling and for action, then we have one left to examine: action.

We shall see that this third method is the most powerful of all, and like Hegel's dialectic includes and subordinates the other two. And it does so because it begins to look like the method of science itself, which employs all three in their proper order, shifting from the domination of one to the domination of the other, until an approximation of the truth stands revealed.

The scene of our continued drama shifts to the United States now, and to a group of Americans who have gone by the name of *pragmatists,* from the Greek word for "practice." Their leader and the founder of their philosophy was Charles S. Peirce (1839-1914). The son of a Harvard mathematician and the first Harvard graduate to receive a bachelor of science degree, Peirce led a difficult life. He taught for a while at Harvard, and later at Johns Hopkins, but for the longest period he worked for the Coast and Geodetic Survey in Washington, and he was surveying the coastline of Louisiana when Darwin's famous book *The Origin of Species* was first published (1859).

Peirce was a philosopher with a strong interest in the method of the physical sciences. His philosophy was colored by this interest. He tried to make a parallel of the scientific method for use in philosophy. He did not quite succeed, but he did succeed in discovering a new approach to philosophical problems.

Peirce was also an American, and Americans, because they were busily building a new country and exploring their frontier lands, had a practical turn of mind. What concerned Peirce was the intimate relation between theory and practice by relating the theory of philosophy to the practice of everyday life. Philosophy in this relation was represented by truth. The way to discover truth is by using the scientific method, the laboratory method of experiment and the field method of close observation.

Once a truth is discovered, the next step is to put it into practice. The truth is what works best in practice and so from the point of view of practice itself, it is best to discover the truth. *What is true will work*. This was Peirce's pragmatic declaration.

But that is not the end of the story. Peirce had a very good friend, acquired in his undergraduate days at Harvard, named William James. William was the brother of the novelist Henry James, and came from a wealthy Cambridge family. William remained for most of his life at Harvard as a professor and divided his time between philosophy and psychology, often doing philosophy from a psychological standpoint.

William remained a life-long friend of Peirce and often helped him financially. He tried hard to understand Peirce's philosophy and to adopt it. But he did not understand fully and so he adopted something like it, which he too called *pragmatism*. But James' version of pragmatism was sharply different from Peirce's. Although he used the same words to describe it, he used them in a different order. Where Peirce had said that *what is true will work*, James declared that *what works is true*.

Words are very tricky things; it is more difficult than we think to make them say exactly what we mean, no more, no less. Although the two statements sound very much alike, they are quite different in meaning, since the one does not convert into the other, and so it should not be too surprising that they led to sharply different kinds of behavior. For Peirce's version led to the laboratory where truths are discovered; James' version led to a particular view of the practical life.

You may remember what the frontier in the western states was like toward the end of the last century. You have seen it in many a movie and read about it in many a novel. Justice was administered in very rough ways. Men were too busy carving out a civilization in the forests and open plains to have time for the niceties of the law. The important thing was to get on with the business at hand. In short they had a philosophy of practice although they did not have any words for it. James, without meaning to, gave them the words. Never mind about truth as such, he seemed to be saying, "if it works it is true." Stick to workability, in other words, and the truth will take care of itself.

This may serve very well for a frontier philosophy and yet not do quite as well for a settled civilization. The influence of the western frontier was felt strongly by those living more conventional lives in the eastern states. It might have misled them if they had followed it too faithfully. Business men always did accept it, but there were others with less special interests who did not.

In the 1920s when Mussolini's "fascists" were in control of the government of Italy, many things that had not worked so well before were made to work for the first time. American business men came back from vacations in Italy, and remarked, "You can say what you like about Mussolini, but he has got the trains running on time."

The pragmatic viewpoint appealed to the "practical-minded man" who was chiefly concerned with the problems of the present moment. The only trouble was that a philosophy which seemed to be working well for the short run did not work for the long run. And it was not many years before pragmatic considerations led Mussolini to take his fascists into an international war which neither he nor they could handle. He ended up hanging by his heels next to his mistress when he was caught by anti-fascist patriots while trying to escape to Germany.

The trouble with the pragmatism of the short run, James'

pragmatism, was that it did not spell out the number of trials needed to assure "workability." As a quick check on the truth of a statement, James' short run version of pragmatism is no help, for it could just as easily give a wrong answer as a right one. How long a time do we need before we can be sure that something works and is therefore a "truth"? Peirce had said that what is true will work, but he too had not spelled out the length of time that would be necessary in order to be sure that the number of trials was sufficient to guarantee a truth.

Like all good scientists, Peirce wished to leave this an open question. Scientists hold all their conclusions, their "laws" and their "facts" forever open to question and subject to revision. Like the ancient Greek skeptics and Stoics, he preferred to talk in terms of percentages rather than in terms of certainties, in terms of the probable truth rather than the "absolute truth." The probable we can know from experience, the absolute as such we can never know.

This difference led Peirce to set up within his system of philosophy a principle which he called *fallibilism*. That is to say, he held out always the possibility that whatever he said might be wrong. A principle of error was necessary in order to avoid making claims that might be too sweeping.

Unfortunately for James, however, actual practice is not like that. There is something absolute and final about every thing that happens, no matter how trivial. If it is a fact that I dropped a book a minute ago, that is a part of my history forever, and nothing I can ever do will change it. Facts are absolute and James had to deal with facts, or at least with a theory about facts. And so he made the mistake of making his theory absolute, too. He stumbled into it, so to speak. And as we have noted, for instance in the case of fascism, it does not "work" too well.

James missed the point that there are intermediate steps between theory and practice, and so he thought that metaphysical theories have no application. But Peirce knew better than that, and we have had since then many elaborate examples of the thesis that James was wrong. Look at the tremendous effects of the metaphysical theory of dialectical materialism (Marxism), look at the fancy metaphysical theories of modern physics, and you will see that the more abstract the theory the greater its effects upon practice once a path has been found leading from the one to the other.

Peirce was on the track of something important, something much more basic. He was trying to discover the fountainhead of reliable knowledge. He thought he had found it in the scientific method. In that method action is the leading edge. Observations and experiments are usually conducted with complex instruments involving many kinds of planned moves, which means that every observation and every experiment requires action. But the other two capacities we have spoken of, the capacities for feeling and thought, are also involved.

And so the scientific method is one that calls out all of the capacities of the entire man. It is the whole man engaged in inquiry. The search for a theory of reliable knowledge seems to have arrived home at last. Unfortunately, the scientific model has not produced the splendid results in philosophy that were expected of it. It has not worked out any better there than it has in the social fields. I think it can be shown that social events are more complex and therefore that it will require a longer time to develop an adequate theory to fit them.

We cannot leave Peirce and pragmatism without saying something about his theory of ethics. Peirce did not live a very conventional life in terms of the values of his day. He was always in some trouble, usually involving women. However, he did hold conventional views respecting religion. He was a pious Protestant Christian and it never occurred to him to question its teachings although he did question nearly everything else. Being an original thinker, he discovered a new way to defend the moral life as he saw it, and indeed developed an argument that he thought would prove its worth.

He saw Christianity very much in the terms spelled out in *Matthew* 22: love God, and love your neighbor as yourself. Without bothering too much with what was meant by God,

184 Knowledge from Action Alone

Peirce thought that he had discovered a logical way of getting from neighbor-love to God by a series of steps which could prove to be the only logical procedure.

Let us begin, he suggested, with the opposite of altruism. Let us suppose a man who is utterly selfish. What does this mean? It means that he will identify his interests only with himself. But that is illogical, because the man knows that he will die. Does he not therefore have to include among his selfish interests at least his wife and children? The answer is obvious: he does. But then will his interest stop there? The welfare of himself and his family is hopelessly bound up with the welfare of all those who live in the same community. All must prosper or fall together.

The community in its turn is not a completely isolated affair. It is part of a wider community, the county, say, and that is part of a state. The state is part of the United States, and the United States is but one nation among the United Nations, and so on until he identifies his interest with the whole of humanity on the surface of the earth.

But as we know now so well, the earth itself is not entirely independent. It revolves around the sun. The solar system is part of a larger system called The Galaxy. And The Galaxy is part of a still larger system of galaxies, until we reach nothing less than the largest community, which is that of the entire universe.

And so beginning with a man who is utterly selfish, we have come to see that to be logical he must extend his interests until he can identify them with the welfare of the universe. But look at what has happened. Egotism has turned into an extreme form of altruism, a concern with the self by a series of unavoidable steps has become a concern for the welfare of others. Peirce's name for his theory of morality was "the unlimited community."

Perhaps the largest lesson of Peirce's theory of the unlimited community is that a man cannot go directly from himself to God. He reaches to God because presumably he thinks that God is the creator of the universe. But the steps cannot be skipped, that is the point. A man has not done enough with love if he loves himself first and then God. Between them he must love his neighbor, and then his neighbor's neighbor, in an unbroken series of loves which gradually widens until it includes the whole of the material universe.

The sequence can best be shown perhaps by an actual example. In the spring of 1929, a friend of mine, the novelist and short story writer Sherwood Anderson made a brief tour of the southern United States, starting in Virginia where he lived, and ending in New Orleans where he loved to visit. He stopped to talk to superintendents in a number of big industries.

In each of them he was told more or less the same thing. "We have just installed a new machine that will do the work of ten men but two men can run it. And so we have let eight of the men go."

"Where will those eight get other jobs?"

"I don't know," was the general answer. "I suppose at some other factory."

But at the next factory he heard the same story, for there the same events had occurred. Suddenly, Anderson had a picture of many men out of work. He realized that all of them had been customers for the products of the factories as well as workers in them. He explained this to the superintendent he met at the next factory he came to. He expected some explanation but all he got was an expression of irritation.

"Look, Mr. Anderson," the superintendent said, "I run my factory as best I can, and that is all. It is none of my business what happens in other factories. I am not my brother's keeper."

That was in the spring of 1929, and Anderson was witnessing the end of a process that had been going on for some time. With millions of men out of work, in the fall of 1929 the great economic depression began. It was destined to last for some years despite everything that President Roosevelt could do to end it. It lasted in fact until the outbreak of World War II in December 1941, when the unemployed went into the army and into the factories which were busily engaged in turning out war supplies.

Pragmatism as a philosophy did not end with Peirce and

James. We have noted that James' pragmatism, although based on a misunderstanding of Peirce's, was the one that fitted best with the frontier practice. And so everyone, including many people who never heard of James' philosophy, or, if they had heard of it, still did not know what it was, agreed with it. The American society of the time was a pragmatic society as James understood pragmatism.

It was James' kind of pragmatism, then, that came so widely to be known. Although no one knew it at the time, this version of pragmatism was upset by the necessity of the government to provide support of some sort for ten million men out of work. But James was not the last pragmatist. The last great one was a man named John Dewey.

Dewey was a pragmatist, though his emphasis and hence his language were quite different. The pragmatism of Peirce was wholly objective. He saw the necessity for men to come to terms with the world in which they lived, since that world is always bigger than they are. Dewey, more of a subjectivist, departed from the grand tradition into which Peirce had led him and turned aside into the subjective by-pass. He brought the subject back into the picture as the equal of the object. Together they made up *experience*, a key word for Dewey as it had been for Kant. Moreover, for Dewey thinking and perceiving are not different and both are parts of experience; curiously, so is the object. It does not exist apart from experience. For Dewey, both the subject of knowledge and the object of knowledge are swallowed up by experience which so to speak makes them both possible.

It has always appealed to subjectivists that if there was no experience of an object, there could be no knowledge of the object, but then they go on to declare that if there was no knowledge of the object there would be no object. The absence of experience does not give them the warrant to assert that. They have clearly confused being with knowing, but they are not one and the same thing. The error has become so common a spectacle on the subjective by-pass that it might almost be called the philosopher's error. We believe in all sorts of things we have never directly experienced, and we do so by reason of inference. At one time this was true of some elementary particles in physics, and it is true now of life on distant planets.

Dewey liked to call his philosophy *instrumentalism*, by which he meant that ideas are the instruments for social action. Society, which is a product of collective thinking, is in a state of continual development. There is no such thing, then, as unchanging "truth" and "goodness," only what evolves of them because they "work," and by "work" Dewey meant work in the present. He was not concerned with the past, only with what holds true today.

Pragmatism, or as Dewey preferred to call it, *instrumentalism*, is a theory of knowledge. Dewey had no interest in any theory of reality, which he ruled out as useless and unnecessary. Reality is experience and everything else falls into it.

Peirce was the great pragmatist. In the hands of his successors pragmatism became something less. Peirce recognized this himself, for when James took over the word, Peirce fell back on another. He began to call his own doctrine *pragmaticism*, which, he said, was "ugly enough to be safe from kidnappers."

Peirce stands out as the greatest of American philosophers, and this is generally acknowledged. His ideas are immensely suggestive, but that is not all. He had a system of philosophy as well, and though he did not present it in a complete work, it has been put together for him. I might try to sketch out the main features of his theories of metaphysics and epistemology.

First, his metaphysics, or theory of reality. Peirce based it on what he thought would be the simplest of all classifications, and named them after the first three numbers, *firstness*, *secondness* and *thirdness*, for the three most elementary properties of the world.

Firstness is *quality*, for quality is simpler than anything else. Peirce meant by this any quality, say the redness of the rose, the bravery of the hero, the hardness of iron, the vagueness of generality.

Secondness is *activity*, which Peirce understood in terms of conflict or resistance. All action is *against* something, for that is the nature of the transfer of energy.

Thirdness is *generality*. Peirce here meant something like a universal law of science, an equation in mathematics, these are thirdnesses.

Every secondness contains qualities, or firstnesses, as parts. Similarly, every thirdness contains both qualities and activities, firstnesses and secondnesses.

My readers will be able to see here a version of Plato and Aristotle, with perhaps a touch of Hegel. Plato's world of Ideas or universals, including sublevels of qualities and mathematical elements; Aristotle's world of matter, containing both qualities and universals involved in a continual activity.

Peirce's theory of reality combined the abstract level of Platonic Ideas with the material level of Aristotle's matter in a way which gave them an equal importance. We live in one and think about the other, and so operate in terms of both. What for Plato were the Ideas or universals, the "intelligible things," Peirce named firstnesses and thirdnesses. And what for Plato were particulars, or "sensible things," Peirce named secondnesses.

The world of secondness (in which qualities and relations are of course heavily imbedded in a complex network), the material world, in which we all exist and strive, is the scene in which three great forces exert their influence continually. These are: *chance, love* and *logic*. Peirce had fancier names for them, but these are more descriptive. Let us look at them one at a time.

Chance (Peirce's name for it was *tychism*) furnished the variety to the world. That is a true qualification to the extent to which laws are never absolutely fulfilled. "All that chance is competent to destroy, it may, once in a long, long time, produce." It is responsible for spontaneity and novelty. It explains conflicts. It accounts for the quality of feeling.

Love (or *agapism*) is the rule of growth through the law of attraction. "Evolutionary love," Peirce called it, for it accounts for the continuous growth of law, and the development of the universe from a state of vague potentiality to one of concrete existence.

Logic (or *synechism*) is the growth of reasonableness, the "doctrine that all that exists is continuous," nothing but "the perfect law of relationship." A true continuity is one which "no multitude of individuals can exhaust," and is therefore infinite.

Now a quick look at Peirce's epistemology, his theory of knowledge. For him it emerged from his theory of signs. Knowing is a kind of sign relationship. If a man perceives an individual object, he is able to do so because of his knowledge of the universal. If the object he sees is a fish, for instance, it is because the name for the universal—"fish"—is a sign to him that the object is related to the universal—in this case "fishness." It is because he is able to remember the classification that he can recognize in the object what it is. "A sign [in this instance the word, *fish*] is anything which determines something else to refer to an object to which itself refers." The sign provokes in the perceiver the more developed sign which is an image. Without the ground, which is the universal, there can be no representation. One big point is that the sign relationship would exist potentially even if there were no one in a position to perceive it at a particular moment.

Complicated, no doubt. To make matters worse, Peirce distinguished sixty-six classes of signs. The whole topic is of immense importance to professionals, especially to logicians, and perhaps now had better be left to them.

Peirce was the greater philosopher though James is better known. But I cannot leave the pragmatists without mentioning one of James' ideas which has influenced quite a few philosophers, Bergson included, and others yet to be mentioned. That was his idea of God and of God's influence in the world.

James thought that just as the world that God had made is imperfect, so God too is imperfect. There is too much pain in the world for God to be happy about it. God, declared James, cannot be happy so long as a single cockroach suffers from unrequited love. God is continually seeking to improve not only the world but Himself. God is God-in-the-making, a conception which has come to be known as "the process God."

So far as belief in God is concerned, James thought that we can control it. We must have a God, as Kant argued, to satisfy our moral and aesthetic needs. And for the purposes of belief we can make the effort, we can "will to believe." Religiously inclined people were drawn to that view of course, but Peirce, religious as he was, opposed it. You can no more will to believe than you can will to doubt, Peirce said. Both belief and doubt he declared are at the service of logic and evidence. You can only believe what there seems to you to be good reason to believe.

Peirce if rightly understood came to restore in the name of the method of the physical sciences the ancient tradition of an independent reason which had been stated and defended along classical lines by Plato and Aristotle. For Peirce, Descartes had been the villain who had led philosophy down the by-pass of subjectivism. Descartes had based his philosophy on the will-to-doubt, which could no more be defended than James' will-to-believe. Descartes, Peirce argued, derived the existence of everything—God as well as the world—from his own consciousness. He made a mystery of religious faith, whereas it is the duty of philosophy to clear up mysteries, not to endorse them.

Peirce did not try to complete his system of philosophy, only to give us the tools by means of which a consistent and comprehensive system could be constructed, and in that lay his strength.

Chapter XIV

The Hidden Philosophy
of Americans

Many years ago I found myself at a rather large dinner party seated next to an elderly and very dignified lady who refused all my overtures at polite conversation. Then, between dessert and coffee she suddenly turned to me and said, in a reproachful tone that suggested she was charging me with a criminal offense, "I hear you are a philosopher."

I admitted the truth.

She drew back and stared at me with unmistakable disapproval. "But," she insisted, "you are too young to be so resigned."

Later it occurred to me that what she was expressing was only a very common attitude inherited from the nineteenth century. We do tend to think of philosophy as some sort of passive contemplation conducted in impotence, a sort of private consolation for public failure. We tell the man who has not succeeded that he should not despair but should learn instead to take his defeat philosophically. Most people understand by philosophy a set of teachers and books gentle in their import but practically powerless. Nothing could be further from the truth. The common misuse of the word "philosophy" conceals the vastness of effects which are subterranean but governing—implicit yet so pervasive as to be rarely detected.

The great power of philosophy is something like this: to give both a driving force and a focus to a sprawling, many-sided society.

A pervasive antiphilosophical attitude has just about prevented the recognition of this fact in the United States. Formal philosophy is not cultivated, nor is its informal presence and power recognized or admitted. Formal philosophy may stagnate and die under the circumstances. Informal philosophy does not advance, but it does not die either. And so a philosophy of the United States does exist, imbedded in our culture as the presuppositions of its practice. Here and there a little exposed philosophy shows above the surface like tiny patches of ground in snow, and when it does we can see what it is, and, perhaps, how it affects the nation.

The philosophy of the United States may be called idealistic materialism. An idealism with regard to the reality of universal truths. A materialism with regard to the reality of particular things.

Idealism credits a superior permanence and reliability to the mind and its contents. Idealism implies a reality of ideas of perfection and of the mind which knows them. There is no distinction in idealism between the independent being of the ideas of perfection (as maintained by Plato, for instance) and the importance of the knowing mind (as maintained by Descartes). A subjective idealism is therefore confused with an objective idealism, and all that is certain is the supremacy of idealism. For subjective idealists the existence of matter is either doubted (as with Bishop Berkeley) or actually denied.

Materialism, on the other hand, insists on the superior reality of matter. The material world of concrete objects in time and space, together with their energy and motion, is all that is important. Man takes part in this world chiefly through his actions. The human mind becomes a kind of secondary or derived affair to which we need assign no great prestige.

Now the curious thing is that the two parts of the American idealistic materialism hardly fit together. Indeed, the situation is worse than that: they are opposed. Idealism asserts the reality of mind over the reality of matter; materialism asserts the reality of matter over the reality of mind.

There is, then, the ever-present danger that the two halves, which live an uneasy life together, will split apart. They do so regularly. The cleavage shows clearly in both the theory of the American thinkers and the practice of the American people throughout the country's history.

In Europe, Bishop Berkeley had insisted that matter is nothing but the complex of our sensations, but the great Sam Johnson had kicked a stone to show that the sensations are caused by something material. The tradition of American thought had shifted back and forth between these opposites. American idealism, which began with the early ecclesiastic authorities, has received formal expression ever since Jonathan Edwards (1703-58). Edwards founded his idealism on European philosophers, on Bishop Berkeley and on Ralph Cudworth and other Neoplatonists. Reality for him was reflected in human thought and in the reality of God's mind. Almost a century later idealism first found its full American voice in Ralph Waldo Emerson. Aided by Berkeleian subjectivism, Emerson developed transcendentalism. He felt obliged to doubt the existence of matter, as the French economist Turgot had advised all competent metaphysicians to do. Emerson's idealism was colored by religious emotion, by intuition rather than by reason. For him the spiritual life was manifested in human existence by the over-soul revealed in man's mind.

Edwards marks the faint beginnings of idealism. Materialism in the United States began in the same period—with Cadwallader Colden (1688-1776). Matter itself, Colden declared, was unknowable, but we could know it through its actions. And he went on to emphasize this phenomenological aspect of action: it is through action that things impinge on our senses. As idealism matured in Emerson, so did materialism become self-conscious with Thomas Cooper (1759-1839). Cooper defended materialism more than he explained it, but he understood matter as active as well as extended, capable in itself of attraction and repulsion.

Materialism was succeeded by pragmatism, a philosophy of experience. Action for Colden was a way of knowing matter. But the pragmatists, who were the new philosophers of experience, were not interested in matter. Action was their touchstone.

We have noted that the man who was responsible for pragmatism was the greatest of American philosophers, Charles S. Peirce. He tried to fuse idealism and materialism. He found a place in the same philosophy for both the logic of ideals and the world of nature. He returned to the Colden concept of action—but this time as part of the meaning of truth. It is possible to accept both the transcendentalism of principles and the naturalism of material events, Peirce suggested, but only if we suppose that both are developing from a world of chance to one of order, and if we insist on learning about principles by the painstaking but reliable method of experiment practiced by the physical sciences.

In the hands of his followers, the two traditions diverged again. William James picked up the materialism and Josiah Royce the idealism. We have already talked about James. Royce, another friend and colleague of Peirce at Harvard, was interested in religion and in his hands Peirce's idea of experience became a sort of infinite experience of the Absolute. And so the materialism and idealism in American philosophy split apart again. No one is trying theoretically to fuse them now.

So much for the career of opposites in the thought of American philosophers. The fact is that every society has a built-in philosophy, an underlying set of ideas whose truth is so taken for granted that they are almost unknown even to those who hold them. In this way a hidden philosophy makes the culture possible, and culture makes an exposed philosophy possible. We get the culture from the ideas which are sufficiently broad as to lie within it unseen and unfelt, and we get the philosophy, which consists in the books and professors, from the culture.

But the philosophy of a culture grows up within it at the

same time that its results occur. Slowly in the social body, through the customs, the institutions, and the loudly proclaimed set of preferences, a central core of general ideas is assembled. No one yet knows the method, and there are no controls. The method, so far as it can be talked about at all, consists in a slow seepage. The rule about philosophy in this sense is that it is never called out by name. It gets into the culture through language, through the arts, through the customs, through the arrangement of institutions, through the contribution of individual men of genius, through other and more subtle means which have not yet been successfully isolated. But the philosophy does circulate, and later on, when we are in a position to see the culture as a whole (which is always some time after it has ceased to exist except in history), we can identify it with some degree of reliability. The professional philosophers reflect the culture. As one might expect, therefore, it is possible to find in social events the same split philosophy.

Our social tradition contains the same conflicting elements: the idealism of Christian piety and adherence, and the materialism of hard work and capital accumulation. You can see the split philosophy at work on Americans in a famous piece of advice: "Trust in God and keep your powder dry," advice which was echoed many years later at Pearl Harbor in "Praise the Lord and pass the ammunition." The successful men in this tradition embody both strains—Rockefeller, for instance, with his philanthropy and his oil properties. The most famous spokesman for this group was much earlier: Benjamin Franklin. The two conflicting elements met in cheerful combination in Franklin. Hard work meant—logically and inevitably—practical success with its resultant health, wealth, and wisdom. Material good followed from material means and the whole thing was suffused by the glow of idealistic righteousness.

Few people today have Franklin's cheery faith. As in theoretical philosophy, the two halves of the tradition have split apart again. In present-day America the alternation of idealism and materialism explains a good deal in the way of irreconcilable policies and practices. It explains the idealism of our foreign policy and the pragmatism of our domestic programs—a foreign policy conducted on the assumption that treaties made with other nations have the inviolability of contracts between individuals under the sanction of state power, and an internal policy that makes the most of individual competition and the struggle for survival. Idealism explains the great revival of interest in religion and the great number of new churches. Materialism explains the production of 7,000,000 cars a year and the enormous vogue for gadgets like radios, electric toasters, and washing machines. The idealism is recognized in the religions subscribed to on Sundays, and the materialism in the business practices that prevail on weekdays: in the spiritual exaltation of the one and the material profits of the other—a heavenly goal, but with cash in the bank.

The alternation of opposites explains our idealistic attitude toward the United Nations and our materialistic preparation for total atomic war.

It is part of our idealism that we insist on proclaiming a high moral code—and part of our materialism that the only real immorality lies in getting caught. It is part of our idealism that when seriously ill we send for the priest and part of our materialism that first we send for the doctor. It is part of our idealism that we are slow to provoke to violence, being reluctant to believe that conflicts cannot be settled short of war, and part of our materialism that we are great fighters. It is part of our idealism that we think well of art—and part of our materialism that we don't think well of artists. It is part of our idealism that a college education is essential— and part of our materialism that we don't think much of colleges.

We are not an intellectual country. At our best we are simply not much interested in ideas. At our worst we are definitely against them. This fact has been noted over and over again—the only argument possible is about the exact degree of interest or opposition.

But what has remained unnoticed is the reason for this disturbing anti-intellectualism. This is the one subject on which the divergent sections of our implicit hidden philosophy, idealistic materialism, agree. Believing as we do, as our unthought-about heritage has led us to do, we must of necessity be anti-intellectual. Idealism insists that there are no *new* intellectual ideas to be advanced. Materialism insists that there are no *important* intellectual ideas. They are slightly different approaches but the implication is clear: things intellectual are things without value.

We think simply because all men are men of good will they can be got to agree; that is our idealism. But we don't think philosophy counts; this is our materialism.

This is the way we are now: in a series of contradictions and with one point of agreement. There are many things in our society that could be better; there are even more that could be far worse. But whatever we are, whatever we think we are, whatever value we set upon our current position, we will want to change, to improve. And for any social change to be permanent or far-reaching in its effect, it must take into consideration our prevailing unconscious attitudes. As unconscious beliefs influence the conscious actions of an individual, so do inherent attitudes influence the actions of a society.

As a people we *do* have a philosophy. We are not conscious of it as the Russians are conscious of theirs. But then theirs is still new. Ours is not. Ours goes so deep we are no longer aware of it. But to be unaware of a thing is not to be uninfluenced by it. We have a deep feeling of insecurity based on the concealed holding of a split philosophy. Our philosophy may be hidden but it is no less operative. It is necessary, then, that we bring the hidden philosophy to light, and heal the split in it by restoring the kind of compromise that Peirce has suggested. If we are to maintain our freedom and our moral authority in the world, it is essential that we become aware of the nature of philosophy and the social power that it is.

Chapter XV

Recent European Philosophy

At the beginning of the twentieth century, the United States came of age. With the first quarter of that century it began to look as though the new pathfinders in the sciences, in the arts, and in philosophy were to come from this country.

While western Europe never surrendered her leadership in the pure sciences, much of applied science and technology originated in the United States, and it is superb. The rest of the world has learned much from her chemists, her physicists and her biologists. In physics the large new instruments that were needed to probe the secrets of the interior of the atom were largely American inventions and constructions.

In the fine arts, a fresh vigor seemed to possess American novelists, while in painting, the new abstractions done by the members of "the school of New York" were widely imitated in Paris and London.

In philosophy, the American pragmatists became important and were exported to Europe where for a brief while their influence was strongly felt. Unfortunately, this part was not to last. American philosophy as an original and vital enterprise died out. After the pragmatists, philosophy moved back to Europe again. Such philosophy as there has been in the United States since that time mostly represents the work of recent Europeans. The most notable for their influence are the following: Kierkegaard, the Dane, and his followers, notably the Frenchman, Sartre, with *existentialism;* the German, Husserl, with *phenomenology;* another German, Heidegger, whose ideas combine those of Kierkegaard and Husserl; and, finally, an Austrian who worked chiefly in England, Ludwig Wittgenstein, with *linguistic philosophy.*

I can tell you in advance that all of them have taken the subjective by-pass. That road over the last couple of centuries, and especially in the last few decades, has grown into an important artery, so much so that it is often mistaken for the main highway, which, however, I insist it is not.

But let us look at the philosophies separately, in the order in which I have named them.

First, then, *existentialism.* Its founder was Søren Kierkegaard, a profoundly unhappy man, unsuccessful in love, uncomfortable in society, and with large feelings of guilt. He led a rather wild life as a student at the University, fell in love with a girl named Regina, whom he renounced. He never married. It would be illuminating to hear Regina's side of the story. Kierkegaard evidently demanded credit for his sacrifice in what he regarded as the name of religion, but what about her? He disliked all of the institutions of his time, not only science and industry but also the Danish State Church which he was busily engaged in denouncing when he died. He was influenced by Hegel but was severely critical of him.

Kierkegaard has been described as a neurotic Hegelian. His start is said to have come from a section of one of Hegel's books entitled "The Unhappy Consciousness." Kierkegaard has been described also as a sour Cartesian, because where Descartes had said, "I think, therefore I am," Kierkegaard substituted, "I hurt, therefore I am." Indeed there was little that Kierkegaard liked.

In a world in which he thought, therefore, that nothing

counted but the human individual (as actor, not as spectator), which is what he meant by his famous phrase, "existence precedes essence," he set about to discover the reality in the situation. Truth, he said, is subjective. In contrast to objective uncertainty, there is subjective certainty. The subject bears the only authentic existence, all else is *inauthentic.*

Man is a free, self-transcending subject, a "knight of faith." By *authentic existence* Kierkegaard meant a deliberate self-commitment to his responsibilities by the free individual. What are his most intimate elements? Kierkegaard saw at once that these would have to be negative, since if they were positive they were apt to be shared by others. And what did the negative mean in individual terms?

Philosophy begins with despair. The most intimate and individual negative feelings anyone could have would be the feelings of anxiety and dread, of fear, the fear of death, which means the loss of all individuality. But the only authentic existence is individual existence, to exist is to be an individual. Hence the title *existentialism* for the philosophy of this school.

Society meant for Kierkegaard losing his individuality by being swept up in the customs of a collective society. For him the philosophers, Hegel in particular, robbed the individual of his concreteness by the substitution of lifeless abstractions. To suffer is to be human.

It is in the solitariness of his position that individual man finds himself. The individual is made real by his decisions. Reality hangs upon the subjective inwardness of the supreme ethical choice; that, more than anything chosen, is what counts, for it is in that moment when he must choose that an individual is most himself.

Two of the three philosophies of the present day which have had the heaviest influence are *existentialism* and *phenomenology.* The first, as we have just noted, was the work of a Dane named Kierkegaard. The second was founded on the writings of Edmund Husserl, the German. If Kierkegaard was the first modern philosopher who mistook the subjective by-pass for the high road, Husserl was the second, and a beauty.

Husserl had a very bad case of subjectivism. Nothing interested him unless it could be shown to be part of the mind or in it. He called his study of consciousness *phenomenology*, a long word which had first been used by Kant to describe appearances as distinct from the reality which lay behind it.

Consciousness is like a set of tentacles attached to objects, and has a second function in which it can be aware of that attachment. Consciousness of an object from the standpoint of self-consciousness means attending to an object, *in*tending it to the exclusion of other objects in an act of concentration which involves meaning. What an object is is what it means to consciousness. The subject does the *meaning*, and it is the object which is *meant*. Objects are therefore nothing more than the sum of their meanings. The qualities of objects are their universals, given to all subjects the same and therefore universal in meaning.

Husserl's method was one he thought involved inner observation. The first step, he said is to trace the most basic element of experience to certain active performances of the *subjective ego*. These are particular, but there is a second step in which the inner observation is not of individual things but of groups of individuals with common characteristics, in which he found meanings.

Indeed psychology was Husserl's main interest, and he saw it as the analysis by the subject of his inner states. So far, so good. But then he sought in it not only his theory of reliable knowledge but also his theory of reality. What consciousness contains of the object is what is real about it. You could if you liked see Husserl's philosophy as a kind of intensification of Kant's, only without Kant's object as it is in itself, unknowable but real, the *noumena*.

Heidegger taught at the University of Freiberg where he was a student of Husserl. When the Nazi Party came to power Husserl, who had a Jewish wife, was dismissed and his Chair given to his pupil. Heidegger flourished under the Nazis. He joined the Party and wrote enthusiastic editorials praising Hitler. This support earned him a promotion to Rector of the University in 1933. He resigned the following year and has lived since in official retirement though he has continued to write.

The downfall of Germany under Hitler in 1945 was the direct result of practicing the wrong philosophy. The overwhelming majority of citizens had surrendered their individual wills to the single will of a solitary leader who led them into a war they could not win. The subjective by-pass here took a cruel turn, and the result may have been the end of German power forever.

Since the defeat of the Germans and the branding of many Nazis as war criminals, there has been a concerted and on the whole successful effort to forget Heidegger's affiliation. Some famous writers owe their consequent neglect to their open approval of Hitler, the great Norwegian novelist, Knut Hamsun, for instance. But Heidegger's reputation has flourished. More books have been written about him than about any other recent philosopher, with the possible exception of Wittgenstein.

Heidegger combined Kierkegaard's existentialism with Husserl's phenomenology, and made a metaphysical interpretation of the result. Kierkegaard had called for a personal philosophy based on negative values, Heidegger supplied them. Husserl had called for a general theory of reality, Heidegger, it is said, produced one. He found it in the meaning of being, but unfortunately by "being" he meant only "human being." Following Kant's *thing-in-itself*, Heidegger proposed his own version of Hegel's *being-in-itself*. Heidegger's term is *Dasein*, a German word meaning *being there*. As with his other master, Kierkegaard, for Heidegger man exists chiefly through his choices. Only man can be said to *exist* in the full sense because only man is aware of his own existence.

However, Heidegger said, man was *thrown* into the world and so he does not have his being, with his own responsibility for free decisions, except in the world. But the world is a meaningful system, with its own bruteness. Man can realize his own possibility only by the manipulation of material tools. His world is a social world, with material interdependence; *being* means *being with*. He is his own past and present, and projects his own future. The last fills him with anxiety and *care*. Fear is specific, but *dread* is general, it has no particular object. By anxiety we are held in suspense between authentic and inauthentic existence, and it is this suspense that we ourselves must break.

It is in fact this anxiety which makes man's existence *authentic*. The fear of death calls for a man to take over his own responsibility, to take charge of his own destiny. Once we investigate being, we find that it must include the examination of non-being, of nothing. Once we have come to face up to the nothingness of death we have got over our dread. Pure being, which is what we have sought all the time, and pure nothingness prove to be one and the same.

It has not sufficiently been noted that these last three philosophers did not produce comprehensive systems. The sciences and their discoveries, the facts and the laws which they have brought to light, do not exist for Kierkegaard, Husserl or Heidegger. Their only concern was with what they considered to be the desperate plight of the individual brought on by his existence in the world.

Some critics have pointed out that while existentialism can be a comfort in a world where the social order seems to be suffering a breakdown, still it is something of a cry-baby philosophy. Samuel Butler, the nineteenth century English novelist and thinker left us some interesting notebooks. In one place he had recorded someone's publication of a book entitled *Is Life Worth Living?* Underneath it Butler had written, "This is a question for an embryo, not for a man."

I have been describing the philosophies which today are the most influential ones on the European mainland. In western Europe they have had something of a vogue, and their fame has spread to the United States. However, the most influential philosopher in the English-speaking world is the Austrian, Ludwig

Wittgenstein. He lived for the greater part of his life at Cambridge University, where he first studied under Bertrand Russell and later taught, leaving England only long enough to fight for the Germans against the British in World War I.

Wittgenstein wrote only two major books, one titled *Tractatus Logico-Philosophicus*, published in his lifetime, the other, *Philosophical Investigations*, which he was still writing at the time of his death in 1951; and each of them gave rise to a school of philosophy. The first book, which was his doctoral dissertation, was responsible for *logical positivism*, an extension of Comte's positivism in terms of the metaphysics of realism, followed by the members of the famous "Vienna Circle," philosophers like Rudolf Carnap and others who fled to the United States to escape the Nazis.

It is in many ways a most extraordinary work, a sort of mystical presentation of logic by means of numbered aphorisms. In it he set the goal of showing the outlines of a *logically-perfect language*, in which the sentences which could be directly verified by facts—physical sentences—would support more abstract sentences. It was a metaphysical construction, from which he ruled out all metaphysics! Despite its peculiarities it still stands as something of a model of the scientific method.

You would be hard put to it to tell that it was the model for a method akin to that of science if you read the positivists who derived their views from it. Worse still, they seem to have understood only its metaphysical bias, not its metaphysical assumptions.

Wittgenstein's second book had an even greater influence than the first, for it created linguistic philosophy, the *philosophy of ordinary language*. Wittgenstein had himself denounced his first book in favor of his second which has a much more psychological affiliation and coloring.

Wittgenstein is justly famous for having turned the attention of philosophers to the importance of language. We deal with the material world, he saw, by means of language. But language at times is difficult and obscures our view. The only way to correct this and restore an uninterrupted view is by means of an examination of language itself. Accordingly Wittgenstein showed us how to undertake an analysis of language through the study of the meaning of ordinary words. *Analytic philosophy*, his followers call it, because they analyze ordinary language. Language is a little like eyeglasses. If yours are dirty they will interfere and obscure your view, but if you clean them you will be able to see much better.

There can be little doubt of the value of such an analysis. If we are to understand the world by means of language, our first task is to put our language in order, for we want to be sure that what we understand is the world and we can do so only with the help of language. We don't want to be waylaid by language itself and so caught up in its obscurities that we never see the world by its means but only the language itself. Yet it is important to remember this can happen to the unwary in the very act of following Wittgenstein's suggestion.

Perhaps I can best explain linguistic analysis by making a comparison with the process of psychoanalysis. If you go to a psychoanalyst for treatment, he will ask you to lie on a couch across from the desk behind which he is sitting. Then he will encourage you to indulge in free association by recalling your earliest memories. If possible by skillful guidance he will help you to locate the episodes in your childhood or even earlier when by the process of association you had emotionally accepted the truth of a false proposition, one perhaps on which your later neurotic difficulties were based. In this way he hopes you will be able to get rid of them. A bad practitioner, however, will not bring you out of it but leave you concentrated on your past and in this manner worse off then you were before.

Wittgenstein was an able analyst of ordinary language, but his followers do not always live up to the example he set. The bad philosopher of ordinary language will make a mistake similar to the one made by a bad psychoanalyst. He will lead you to turn your attention to the language you use and he will leave you there concentrated on it. But in this way you will never get an unobstructed view of the world, only a view of the language. He will leave you dependent upon the language you use much in the way the bad psychoanalyst will leave you dependent upon your own past—and upon the psychoanalyst.

Wittgenstein was concerned with philosophy and therefore with the help the study of language could be to it. His followers, alas, or at least most of them, have turned this around. They are more concerned with language and the help philosophy can be to it. In this way they somehow cancel the good effects which ought to follow from Wittgenstein's studies. The absolute disciple, who is a kind of fanatic, the one who supposes that the master could not have been wrong about anything, usually succeeds only in betraying him by exaggerating both his meaning and his claims in such a way as to make only a caricature of his ideas.

Of course we want to be sure that our words have a necessary reference, and we want to know this as much in the case of abstract words, which are the names of classes, as we do in the case of concrete words, which are the names of particular things. And we want to follow meaning as it emerges from the process whereby words are built into sentences and sentences into paragraphs. And then we want to see what the passages indicate without getting lost in or held up by the language we are using.

Language is both the oldest and the most complex of all the tools possessed by the human species. It is so old that nobody has been able to trace the first language, which must have been spoken and not written, and it is so complex that nobody knows the whole vocabulary of any modern language. There are more than 500,000 words in the Oxford English Dictionary, and no one individual could tell you the meaning of all of them. No wonder, then, that the linguistic philosophers have called our attention to the problem of understanding the language we all use so frequently, and in many instances so carelessly.

The heritage which Wittgenstein's followers have interpreted to us is that of a man whose preoccupation with language was entirely in psychological terms. What can language tell us about the mind, about consciousness, about other minds? These are important questions, no doubt about it, but they should not be investigated to the exclusion of other more traditional questions, such as the nature of the physical world, the place of organisms in it, the character of man himself; also such further questions— some of them Kant's—as for instance why are we here (in the world), what should we do (to other persons and things), what dare we hope (about ourselves and the world in which we live), and, finally, what can we learn by considering that all of our knowledge belongs together in some sort of system?

The importance of Wittgenstein to his many followers today need not blind us to the fact that his final reputation may be a somewhat more modest one. Already, Kierkegaard, who was the hero of philosophy in the earlier part of this century, has faded considerably. In the long run a philosophy can survive only if it has something to contribute to the average man. In these terms, unfortunately the linguistic philosopher can say to him only "Watch your language!" and the existentialist can tell him, "You're in one hell of a fix!" Herbert Spencer was an important philosopher a bare hundred years ago, and yet scarcely anybody reads him today and few know even who he was. It can happen again. The passage of time, with its gift of greater detachment and perspective, often reverses contemporary judgments, topples the mighty and raises the fallen, though this is not necessarily the rule. There is no rule in this area, or, if there is, we do not yet know what it is.

I cannot in all justice leave these eminent contemporary philosophers of the subjective by-pass without adding a word about the leading contemporary French philosopher, Jean-Paul Sartre. Sartre has had a vogue in his own country. He was a leader of the French underground during the German occupation in World War II, and he has been a successful playwright and novelist. In this way he has become known to many who might not otherwise have paid any attention, because his philosophy is not easy for the unprepared to read, no easier, say, than the philosophies of his mentors, Hegel, Kierkegaard and Heidegger.

If I say that apart from their ideas there is nothing new in his work, I will find many to disagree with me. He has an engaging approach, and, like the earlier French philosopher Henri Bergson, he has an eloquent literary style. Nevertheless, I can find nothing in him that I cannot find also in the work of his predecessors. Lately, he has introduced one novelty, but it is more concerned with strategy than with original thought. He has embraced Marxism, and this despite the fact that the Marxists have not in return embraced him. Existentialism, his own philosophy, he has declared, is an enclave inside Marxism, a personal philosophy inside the more sweeping claims of a social philosophy, and no less so because the Marxists reject it.

Chapter XVI

The Revival of Realism

The subjective by-pass that we have been examining in the last chapter has been the high road taken by philosophers for some time. But its travellers do not represent all the philosophy there is to-day. For one thing they do not represent Marxism. For another thing they do not represent realism. We have looked long and hard at Marxism in a previous chapter. Let us look briefly now at those modern philosophers who call themselves *realists*.

When I refer to philosophical "schools," it sounds either like a university where a group of men taught together or like a private club to which they all belonged. It means of course no such thing, only that a number of men discovered a common set of ideas at about the same time and may or may not have influenced one another.

Realism is not a new philosophy in the world. It was the philosophy of Plato and Aristotle. It fell into disfavor when science arose and was mistakenly thought to be opposed to it. It was the American realist, Peirce, who first called our attention to the fact that science *requires* realism. Before we can look at the evidence, however, perhaps we might examine modern realism a little closer, see how it arose and what it is.

Let us begin by returning to the scepticism of Hume. He said, if you will recall, that on the basis of sense experience no evidence could be found to justify a belief in the independent reality of the external world. Kant had answered Hume by proceeding to construct a system of knowledge without including the external world which he allowed to remain unknowable.

Some philosophers have thought that they could not accept Hume's position. One in particular, Thomas Reid, the leader of the Scottish school of philosophy, fell back upon *common sense*. It was the lesson of common sense, he said, to accept the existence of an external world which is independent of our experience of it. No one in his ordinary life believes that the world ceases to exist when we stop perceiving it. Common sense dictates that we perceive directly the real objects in the external world, moreover that we perceive them as they actually exist and not as copies of them in our minds. This is the position of realism and Reid argued that we should accept it in theory since we already accept it in practice. Let us be guided by what common sense tells us, he said, and what we believe as a matter of fact, anyway.

Reid and his followers used common sense in a most uncommon way, for most of those who appeal to common sense are not aware that they are doing so, and in any case do not raise it to the abstract level of a philosophy. Nevertheless Reid was on to something, and we can trace his influence, which is still very much with us.

Reid had a follower named Cook Wilson who did not write much, but Wilson had a student named G. E. Moore who did, and Moore had a student named Bertrand Russell. Through that line of philosophers the position was revived that the ancient Greeks had maintained: there *is* an external world of matter. According to Russell's early philosophy there is also in the external world a set of logical types, or universals, *logical atoms,* he called them.

That was his early position. Later, he rejected it. Russell was easily influenced, immensely clever, showed exquisite taste in his borrowings, but was mercurial in his development. If you want to say what Russell's philosophy is you have to date it, because he changed his mind from time to time. But in the period of which we are speaking of he believed in what he called *subsistent entities*, relations between material objects which are like universals, and which do exist independently of our knowing them.

This was not far from the Greek position. It was more like Aristotle's view than Plato's, because Russell did not suppose that there are *two* external worlds, a world of material objects and a world of Ideas, as Plato did, but instead put them together. It was Russell's friend and early collaborator, Whitehead, who took that next step.

Alfred North Whitehead was an English mathematician, born in 1861, the son of an Anglican clergyman. For most of his life he taught at Cambridge University where he had been educated, and he did not begin to write philosophy until toward the end of the first world war. That would have been about 1918, when he was 57 years old. In 1924, when he was 63 he accepted an appointment to the philosophy department of Harvard University where he spent the remainder of his life. It was in his later years at Harvard that he wrote those books which present the world with a system of philosophy which has been called by one scholar, Professor Victor Lowe, "the ultimate intellectual achievement of the nineteenth century." Whitehead's own name for it was "the philosophy of organism," to indicate that while he thought that previous systems of philosophy had been influenced by physics, his was influenced by new developments in biology.

Philosophy when it came to him late in life was not altogether the new interest it seems to have been. Collaborating with Bertrand Russell he had produced from 1910 to 1913 three large volumes of a new mathematical logic, to which they gave a Latin name, *Principia Mathematica*. The topic was so new that type had to be cast for nearly all of the symbols—and it was written almost entirely in symbols. The symbols themselves were the work of an Italian logician, Giuseppe Peano.

The ideas expressed in the book came from two sources. Whitehead brought to it his own ideas, set forth in a previous work on *Universal Algebra*. Russell in characteristic fashion brought those of a German logician, Gottlob Frege, whose work might have been lost if Russell had not called attention to it. Russell as a matter of fact was pretty good at promoting the important but often neglected ideas of other people.

Russell lived in a period of great ferment. He worked in logic, but even more drastic changes had started to come in physics. At the end of the nineteenth century and the beginning of the twentieth the world received the great shock occasioned by science's overthrow of common sense and the introduction of an entirely new system of ideas in physics. It has been slow in seeping down to the level of understanding of the average man, though no doubt a new common sense will eventually issue from it.

Once again a revolution in ideas was led by physics. Many researchers contributed to it, but I will mention here the names only of the two greatest. Max Planck discovered that matter consists in packets of energy. Matter and energy are interconvertible, according to a well-known formula. Einstein discovered that space and time are coordinates and that both are functions of matter-energy. There is no absolute space and time, space-times being determined by the velocity of matter. There is more to it than that of course. A great many old notions went overboard, and all our conventional ideas are in process now of being reconstituted.

The philosopher who tried the hardest to cope with the new ideas in physics by constructing a system of philosophy which would be compatible with them (though by no means limited to them) was Alfred North Whitehead.

Whitehead's philosophy is the last one I shall trouble you about, and also the most difficult. I have saved the hardest for last, because I thought that by now you might be better able to tackle it. One of the difficulties in the way of understanding

Whitehead is that he coined his own words, which means that you have to learn a new vocabulary in order to read him.

Whitehead's philosophy begins with an attack on the older version of common sense. What we regard as unquestionable he said is simply not even true. It is based on the old philosophy which we inherited from Descartes, Locke and Newton. From Descartes we inherited the distinction between mind and matter, from Locke the notion that the secondary qualities (the sense qualities of color, odor, hardness, etc.) belong to the subject and not to the object, and from Newton that matter consists in static bits which stand by themselves in space and time and are only accidentally connected with each other, and that energy is somehow something which acts on bodies by means of motion, not something composing them.

This scheme has been upset and replaced by modern physics with its conception of matter as "sheer activity" or bundles of energy, and by the relativity of space and time. Whitehead argued that any new scheme would have to be consistent with the new findings in physics, and he proceeded to construct one.

The world is composed of material objects—Whitehead called them *actual entities*—and there is nothing else. Only, we must remember that the substance of which the actual entities are composed is highly complex and highly volatile, and that among the actual entities we can count biological organisms and the wholes of which they are parts (their societies), for these too are material objects. Organizations of actual entities are themselves actual entities. Whitehead's name for them is *nexūs*. All actual entities are organizations of various degrees of complexity, and diversity of function is a product of diversity of organization. Also, *events* are actual entities, a proposal which agrees with modern physics in which matter and energy are interconvertible. The world, then, is an *extensive continuum* of events having *extensive connections* (overlappings).

There are no longer any merely local happenings, no strictly limited regions of activity. According to Whitehead, everything is connected with everything else, and all relations are internal to the universe as a whole. Every actual entity is subject to continual modification of the whole by its parts. Qualities and relations are names for large collections of resemblances, such qualities as redness, hardness, sweetness, and such relations as mathematical entities. As classes (or universals) they represent the "primary types of things," the patterns or configurations which recur.

Actual entities perish sooner or later, that is to say, they disintegrate into their component parts. But their qualities and relations do not. Whitehead recognized this permanence by calling them *eternal objects*. Actual entities are composed of sets of eternal objects together with the date and place for their assemblage. There are many similarities among the eternal objects, and groups of them are ranged in tiers the one above the other. The realm of eternal objects consists in just such an arrangement. Together they stand as possibilities forever.

The realms of actual entities and eternal objects are themselves related. Every actual entity is attracted to every other actual entity in a positive way which Whitehead described by the word *prehension*, which means a kind of "grasping." Of course to prehend any actual entity is *not* to prehend all of the others, and this negative side of prehension which excludes the others Whitehead named *negative prehension*, which is the source of logic.

The realm of actual entities is immersed in time, Whitehead declared, hence every actual entity changes continually. It changes by giving up some of its eternal objects and acquiring others. The process of acquisition was named by Whitehead *ingression*; the eternal objects *ingress* into the actual entities. As Whitehead said, instead of the forms of process we have the procession of forms.

Every actual entity has a *subjective aim*. It exists in the mode of *presentational immediacy* (awareness) or in the mode of *causal efficacy* (material causation). It is one of the novelties of Whitehead's philosophy that every actual entity has a subjective aim, that such an aim is not the exclusive prerogative of human individuals. In the human individual admittedly the subjective aim is raised to a degree of intensity we call consciousness and even self-consciousness. But the subjective bias is got rid of by the theory that consciousness is merely a special case of a general situation. Whitehead avoided the subjective by-pass not by denying subjectivity but by attributing it to every actual entity, which is to say to every material organization.

In the Cartesian view all readings are taken from the perspective of the human mind, but now it is the body from which we want our readings to be taken, declared Whitehead, a body which contains not only the physical properties but the mental as well, not only the sensory end organs but the whole of the central nervous system with its brain and its capacity for sensitivity of awareness, for the mind is part of the body and so equally a part of nature.

What we mean by the self (or soul), then, is the stream of experience which somehow centers on an identity. Hence the self (or soul) relies upon the external world to furnish its contents. It does not produce them but only shapes them into a unity.

One of the novelties in Whitehead's scheme is that while actual entities change more or less rapidly, the eternal objects change slowly, from cosmic epoch to cosmic epoch. Whitehead never said how long a cosmic epoch lasts, but since he was talking about astronomical time presumably he meant billions of years. In relation to the realm of actual entities the eternal objects seem not to change at all, which is why they have earned their name of eternal—*eternal* objects.

The realm of eternal objects and the realm of actual entities are both aspects of God's nature. The eternal objects are called collectively the *primordial* nature of God and the actual entities are called the *consequent* nature of God. In this way Whitehead worked God into his metaphysical scheme though it seems to stand just as well without such a conception.

Whitehead's metaphysics invites a comparison with Plato's,

although Whitehead's has been considerably modified by the findings of modern physics. For instance, where Plato had a realm of *Ideas*, Whitehead had one of *eternal objects;* and where Plato had a realm of *material objects*, Whitehead had a realm of *actual entities*. Unlike Plato, for Whitehead the two worlds were equal in reality; and unlike Aristotle (while we are making comparison) for Whitehead there were two realms rather than only one. Whitehead's *eternal objects* are separate and distinct and change slowly, while Plato's *Ideas* did not change at all but were fused in an infinite continuum which is everywhere dense.

Chapter XVII

Problems, Problems, Problems

In the course of the foregoing pages in which I tried to explain philosophy and you have tried to understand it, I know we have been through some very trying times together. Did you notice by the way that the presentation was graded and that the earlier pages gave a simpler picture than the later ones? The words used became more technical as you went along. I wrote it that way so that by the end you might be brought to the point where you could read the writings of the philosophers themselves and not just a book about them.

Books that were fun to write are not always fun to read. I hope this one is. The passion for knowledge for its own sake and not merely for the other benefits it may bring with it is one to be encouraged. That passion has been responsible for all of the ideals we live by and also for all of the material tools we use, for the way we do things as well as for what we do, for ski-parties as well as for skyscrapers, for music as well as for masonry.

Remember when you try to understand a philosophy and run into trouble not to be easily discouraged. The effort will be rewarding, for it may intensify and deepen your understanding of everything else. If it does that, it will also increase your pleasure in living. There is no genuine substitute for true understanding. If you have begun to see how philosophy may be approached, then the reading of this book will have been worth your while. I hope it was, anyway.

This may be the best place to make a very important point, because it comes at the end. Not all philosophers will agree with my version of the classic philosophies. I might even say that none will altogether. But then you must remember that they do not agree with each other, either. I lay it down as a principle that there is no statement in philosophy about which all philosophers can be got to agree—including this statement itself.

Therefore I feel safe in confessing that this account was written from my own point of view. How valuable that point of view is, or isn't, only the test of time can tell. And even the judgment of time is no absolute judgment. Plato and Democritus were rivals. Evidently their contemporaries thought highly of both of them. Yet we have all twenty-eight of Plato's dialogues, and while Democritus is said to have written sixty books, none has survived. Is this a judgment of value? It would certainly seem not.

Is there such a thing as progress in philosophy? Can you look back on the history of philosophy and see that the explanations have become more inclusive? I doubt it. And yet there may have been progress. Not that each philosophy is more inclusive than the one that went before—though that, too, perhaps. For there has been much new knowledge to include, and systems of philosophy have to be above all inclusive. This has become especially true in the last century when scientific knowledge has increased so enormously.

There is no shortage of problems. Without Kant we might not have known that *how* a system of philosophy is held can be almost as important as *which* philosophy is held. Without Hegel we might never have known that circular reasoning could produce results not obtainable by other kinds of reasoning. Take language for instance. Plato discussed the problem of language in one of his dialogues. But it was Wittgenstein who taught us that language is a *method* of communication which if not used properly can be an *obstacle* to communication.

A very wise friend of mine once said to me, in some despair, that if we do not solve the fundamental problems at least we refine them. Progress consists in understanding them better. If we have learned that the kinds of problems philosophy tackles are not the kind to be solved easily or quickly, that *is* a kind of progress, isn't it?

That there is a great deal of new knowledge which will take time to assimilate does not mean that there are no lessons in the old masters. From Socrates, for instance, it is still possible to learn. He said in effect that we know nothing with certainty except that nothing certain is known. Much of our troubles and many of our wars come from thinking that we have the absolute truth and wishing to impose it on others. Yet there are so many different "absolute truths" that the future looks as hopeless and as violent as the past.

The more intelligent people are, the better they are able to get along without having to rely on absolute answers. The only absolute truth about the world is that there are no absolute truths. To understand that and to be able to accept it is progress of a sort. Absolute truth belongs only to mathematical equations. (If you will look carefully at this paragraph, you will see that it contains nothing but absolute truths. You see how very difficult philosophy is?)

What you have to learn how to do, if you wish to follow philosophy by reading it on your own, is to see and be able to recognize the same areas no matter what language is used to refer to them, and this whether they are material things or abstract things, individuals or universals. For the language changes from period to period. A person trained in philosophy for instance would know that what Plato meant by the "dialectic" was not what Marx meant, and that a "Platonic Idea" or "universal" is not the same as an idea or thought in recent philosophy. He would have to see that *thought, feeling* and *action* could be called *reason, sensation* and *behavior,* with the only change being one of perspective.

Philosophies are quite distinct from each other but just to confuse you, it happens that philosophers use either the same words with different meanings or different words with the same meanings. And they do this not out of whimsy but because they are thinking vaguely in terms of comprehensive systems no matter how small the topic under consideration is. What you must practice how to do—and I admit it is not easy—is to see *through* the language they use and *by means of it,* and not get stuck in the language itself.

We have noted that in the early Greek years of its beginning philosophy was free. It was not tied to any particular institution, not to the church, not to the state, not to anything or anyone. But then, you remember, in the Middle Ages it became subordinate to religion. Christianity came first, or Judaism or Islam—Jesus or Moses or Mohammed—while Plato, Aristotle and the other philosophers made a bad second. With the rise of the experimental sciences, particularly the physical sciences, philosophy was liberated. Those philosophers who wished to consider philosophy less important than science were free to do so, but the thing was that they did not have to.

Still, the medieval association of philosophy with religion as its handmaid has persisted. And so before philosophy once more can resume its rightful place, it will have to become dissociated in the public mind from religion. No one will take it seriously until it does. There is a philosophy of religion, granted, but it is no more important than, say, the philosophy of law or the philosophy of education, or the philosophy of anything else.

Religion is after all a kind of mythologized metaphysics, and every religion has a philosophy which is employed in its defense. Yet philosophy itself is broader than that, and since the older religions have lost their credibility what we might look to philosophy for now is a new religion. Everything, every enterprise, has its philosophy, but philosophy as such—an independent philosophy, all off by itself in the morning—comes first.

With the collapse of religion and the rise of science, there is a general feeling on the part of many that they have been left without a base. For the scientists and their followers, reason and fact are sufficient guides because they are the only reliable ones. But there are those who cannot follow such developments. Civilization in this respect has outrun its vast populations.

The light of reason often is a light which is too strong for some to use. They find it easier to accept the irrational and with Tertullian to "believe what is absurd." Hence the popularity of drugs, mysticism, astrology, psychedelics, orgone boxes, flying saucers, ouija boards, the *I Ching* and Tarot cards.

None of these substitutes can gain a general ascendancy; each consoles a few. As I have shown much earlier, belief is comforting and faith is only a strong sort of belief, a belief backed by emotional acceptance. Belief is the cheapest thing in the world. People have at one time or another believed almost everything. By the Indian maharajas, for instance, it was believed that tiger fat cured rheumatism. Elephant hairs are often worn to ward off arthritis. Crossing under a ladder is considered to cause bad luck.

Science effectively destroyed religion, but the material successes of applied science were not enough to satisfy the emotional needs of the masses. They have not understood the spiritual nature of pure science, which seeks only to discover the nature of things, and they are not content with the triumphs of applied science and technology even though their standard of living and their life expectancy has been considerably raised thereby. Left without a faith, they grope for one. They look to the mystic cults, to astrology, and to the oriental religions to supply the missing emotional elements. And they look in vain. The age cries out for a new and acceptable religion, one which could be compatible with the findings of science without being limited to them. And that is where we are today.

The effect of the rapid and astonishing success of the physical sciences has been to make philosophers timid. They pretend to interpret science when what they do is misunderstand it. They undertake small piecemeal investigations because that is what they think the scientists do in their laboratories, ignoring the great systematizers of physics, men like Newton and Einstein.

Philosophy is the result of the attempt to understand the human predicament in its final terms. No one would undertake anything so far-reaching as a fundamental inquiry of this sort if he did not think that it would be a success. The story of philosophy is a sad and a brave one; sad because it was doomed from the start to be a theoretical failure, brave because it has been a practical success.

I think we cannot ever learn anything truly about the answers to the questions the philosophers have always asked. We are here, but in any case briefly, and always without knowing why. Some of the unsatisfactory results of the efforts to reach final answers to the ultimate questions that philosophy is forever asking have been regarded outside philosophy as absolute truths and employed to guide individual careers and establish social institutions. Philosophy has failed to answer the ultimate questions, but its failures have been employed to run countries. The answers the great philosophers have given have even served as the foundations of civilizations.

This is a paradox which has not been recognized, yet it may be a sufficient justification to continue the philosophical pursuit. That we are forever doomed to seek the answers to unanswerable questions may be a good description of the human predicament.

Everyone has a philosophy without knowing it, one which he holds so deeply that he thinks, feels and acts in the world by means of it without even being aware of its existence. To understand philosophy in any full sense each of us must be able to exchange the philosophy he holds for another one, at least long enough to see how the world seems in terms of it.

Philosophy, in other words, is a way of looking at the world, and the philosophically astute person is equipped to try philosophies on until he finds one that fits him. When one looks at things Kantianly, for instance, one sees them in relation to oneself. When one looks at things Platonically, one compares them to the ideals at which *they* aim. And when one looks at things Hegelianly, one sees them as parts of a grand design in which only the total is real. It may be the philosophy one started with as a result of the way one was raised and educated, or it may be a different one.

In any case the opportunity for a comparison is a serious necessity. And the extent of the philosophy one is capable of assuming is a measure of the depth of one's penetration of the world. In every attempt written or unwritten to make a social institution or a government permanent by agreeing on a set of principles as to its aims and purposes and the manner in which it shall be run, there is a philosophy hidden. The only remedy possible against false beliefs is to recognize philosophies behind the exaggerated claims of such social institutions as churches and governments, and to remember that philosophies are largely guesses at the truth by imaginative and thoughtful men who themselves did not regard their work as necessarily complete, consistent or final.

The "liberal" is the modern version of the older humanist. He wishes to count every individual human life as precious and worthy of preservation, along with every political liberty and every economic advantage which would be necessary to a decent and reasonably happy way of life. Who could quarrel with that? I share his hopes.

If I differ with him at all, it is because I think they are only hopes, while he reads what he hopes for as though it were already a fact. He will not face the paradox of human life, which is that human nature has two incompatible sides. Man wishes to help and hurt his fellow man. There has been no progress in motivation since cave man days. He is aggressive because he was trained to be so through 30,000 years of nomadic existence when hunting was his only way of life.

Those who have a desire only for peace and the arts of peace represent a valid side of human nature. The only trouble is that those who have a desire for war and conquest do too. These two sources of human nature come into permanent conflict; one can be satisfied only at the expense of the other. Neither believes the other necessary but in this both are wrong. That is the human problem essentially, and we have come nowhere near solving it.

The recent conversion to settled communities—astonishingly only some 10,000 years old—has brought strains and problems with it. As long as there have been human beings there have been serious conflicts. But crowding men into cities without removing from them their old aggressive tendencies makes large-scale wars inevitable.

The horrible truth is that if peace does not satisfy all of man's needs, war does not, either; evidently he must have both. If this is not true then we have not explained why wars are so common, common not only in the remote past or even in the recent past but in our own day—right now, in fact.

That is a hard fact for the liberal to accept. Gandhi's program of non-violence was followed at the partition of India by the savage slaughter of Moslems and Hindus on the border between India and the new state of Pakistan. Such savagery is not confined to religion though it certainly is widespread among religious people. Men behave in the same way for economic gain, whether they be capitalists or communists.

Before we can get a lovely, peaceful world, we must recognize that the obstacle to its achievement is not something which is very far away from us but human nature itself. Man is the wolf of man, the old Roman saying had it. Until we can change that, or find another outlet for the destructive side of human aggression, we will not have the kind of world we want—want, that is, when we are feeling peaceful.

Only the application of the truth can save us in the end. But until the truth is known, the terms and conditions necessary to its pursuit must be preserved and protected. The *professor* of philosophy in the colleges and universities has the task of all educators. He must preserve and pass on to a coming generation the best of what has been learned in the past. The *philosopher* has a different task, and in many ways a more difficult one. He must add something to what past philosophers have accomplished. He must make *discoveries* in philosophy.

For although much has been preserved that is good, new information and new problems have arisen as civilization has accumulated more knowledge, and with the great increases in population, more problems. Many of our current difficulties arise from the fact that we are products of small societies and still belong to them, whereas through new kinds of communication and transportation, new methods of manufacture, we are reaching for new political organizations capable of coping with an international global society.

In order to be a philosophy teacher or a philosopher, a person must also remain aloof from the contemporary world. He can learn from it—indeed he should learn from it—but he should not seek to influence it. Experience has taught us that there is no such thing as useless knowledge, though there may be a long interval of time between the discovery of a set of truths and the discovery of ways to apply them. Thus what seems at the time like irrelevance may yet contain something of great value. The influence of the philosopher should be directed toward the future, toward that unborn perfect audience which awaits his work after he is dead.

To be a philosopher in the full and true sense, he must remain as unattached and as unaffiliated as he possibly can arrange to be. He must stand apart from anything that might limit his vision or detract from that pure standpointlessness which is his greatest asset and his most precious heritage. That is not as easy to do as to say. Detached inquiry does not come easily because the philosopher lives at ground level, with his local interests and involvements; and yet it is necessary. For the more broadly he sees things the more likely he is to add to human knowledge in a way which will make it a possession forever.

It is a mistake to confuse theory with practice. The practitioners may think they are following the theory, and they even may mean to, and yet end up somewhere very far from it. This surely is the case with Marxism. The Soviet Union and Communist China today are the scenes of the greatest concentration of power and despotism since the absolute monarchies and imperialism of an earlier day. The leaders of those countries which have effected a communist revolution run rigid and ruthless dictatorships in which differences of opinion are not tolerated. Under Stalin those who opposed him simply disappeared and were probably murdered. Under Brezhnev they were sent to mental hospitals, on the theory, I suppose, that whoever differed with the policies laid down by the Supreme Soviet in the Kremlin must be insane!

The communists say, "The capitalists oppress, we liberate." Many have followed them only to find that the liberators practice even crueller forms of oppression. There is nothing in Marxist theory to suggest that the political rulers should be the judges of what is and what is not good in literature and the arts generally, and of what is and what is not true in the sciences.

Philosophy, at least that small part of it which is the possession of the professional philosophers, is society's investment in its own future. The thinker is usually a failure as a man of action—both Plato and Marx were, to take two extreme types—and in any case it is always too late for changes at such a fundamental level. The philosopher ought never to seek to improve the social conditions of his own times. They can only be improved slowly, allowing ideas to seep down into the social fabric where their effects will be felt.

As I leave the writing of this book, it is with considerable apprehension, however. No one who looks at the state of the world could feel otherwise. The frequency of wars and the threat of a greater war conducted with nuclear weapons is frightening and a challenge to the future of the human species. Perhaps we do not deserve to survive, but in any case if we do not we will have been the engineers of our own destruction.

Peace with liberty is not a product of absolute pacifism. It is only a way of achieving peace at any price, and the price might well be subservience to a country which does not practice pacifism. I am afraid of the disastrous social effects of those idealists who know very well where they want us to go but do not know how to get us there.

I cannot help loving what is good in my fellow-man, and there is a lot of good in him. I for one wish him to survive, and if only he will learn how to plan his future a little better and how to adhere to his plans a little more, he may survive. Yet philosophy, which in the end is nothing more than the search for the truth about the nature of things, and without which nothing lasting can be done, is still only a hope.

Acknowledgments

The quotations from Socrates, Antisthenes and Aristippus, freely adapted, are from Diogenes Laertius, *Lives of Eminent Philosophers* (London, 1925, Heinemann), 2 vols.

The quotations from Philo are from the translation by F. H. Colson and G. H. Whitaker (London, 1949, Heinemann), The Loeb Classical Library, 11 vols., vol. I, "On The Creation," pp. 153-6.

Chapters I and XIII appeared first as essays in *The Saturday Review*.

Readings for Continued Study

Angell, Norman, *The Great Illusion*, 1908.

Butler, E. M., *The Tyranny of Greece Over Germany* (Cambridge, 1935, University Press).

Clark, Grahame, *World Prehistory*. (Cambridge, 1969, University Press).

Frankfort, H. and H. A., and others, *Before Philosophy* (Baltimore, 1951, Penguin Books).

Fuller, B. A. G., and McMurrin, S. M. *A History of Modern Philosophy* (New York, 1955, Henry Holt).

O'Leary, De Lacy, *How Greek Science Passed to the Arabs* (London, 1948, Routledge and Kegan Paul).

Toynbee, Arnold J., *A Study of History*. (London, 1934, Oxford University Press). There have been many different editions of this work.

Wolfson, Harry Austryn, *Religious Philosophy* (Cambridge, Mass., 1961, Belknap Press of Harvard University Press).

Index